CONNECTING
to the FUTURE

A Blueprint for Dynamic Leadership

MOHAMMED ALARDHI

SIMON ELEMENT

New York   London   Toronto   Sydney   New Delhi

**SIMON
ELEMENT**

An Imprint of Simon & Schuster, Inc.
1230 Avenue of the Americas
New York, NY 10020

First Simon Element hardcover edition October 2023

SIMON ELEMENT is a trademark of Simon & Schuster, Inc.

For information about special discounts for bulk purchases, please contact Simon & Schuster Special Sales at 1-866-506-1949 or business@simonandschuster.com.

The Simon & Schuster Speakers Bureau can bring authors to your live event. For more information or to book an event, contact the Simon & Schuster Speakers Bureau at 1-866-248-3049 or visit our website at www.simonspeakers.com.

Manufactured in the United States of America

1   3   5   7   9   10   8   6   4   2

Library of Congress Cataloging-in-Publication Data has been applied for.

ISBN 978-1-6680-3288-6
ISBN 978-1-6680-3289-3 (ebook)

To the men and women of Investcorp,
with gratitude and appreciation.
You inspire me every day.

CONTENTS

MOHAMED A. EL-ERIAN

first became aware of Investcorp back in the 1980s, when I happened to share a ride from Heathrow Airport to the Oxford Energy Conference with Nemir Kirdar, Investcorp's founder. At the time, I was working at the International Monetary Fund and knew nothing about Investcorp. But I quickly learned.

Nemir explained that Investcorp had been founded a few years earlier with the idea of providing a bridge between long-term capital from the Arabian Gulf countries and investment opportunities in the United States and Europe. I thought it was a good thing for the Gulf and international capital markets to link up better. Purely by coincidence, I had written my doctorate thesis a few years earlier about the good, the bad, and the ugly of the recycling of petrodollars, but I had taken mainly a public sector angle. Now here I was sitting in a car with someone who was actually doing it in the private sector.

Over the ensuing years, I noticed Investcorp when it made headlines for big acquisitions like Gucci, Saks Fifth Avenue, and Tiffany. But I had no direct contact with the firm for decades, until I was seated next to Mohammed Alardhi at a dinner at a conference in Abu Dhabi in the mid-2010s.

I was intrigued by how, at the young age of thirty-one, Mohammed had become the head of the Royal Air Force of Oman. I was impressed when he told me what he had accomplished at the RAFO. I asked him about his career since leaving the military, and it was only then that he told me that he had recently become Executive Chairman of Investcorp. I told him about my encounter with Nemir Kirdar, and he started sharing his vision of transformation for the firm.

I remember him telling me something along the lines of "Yes, we're going to continue to be a bridge for private capital from the Gulf to the rest of the world. But rather than rest on our laurels, we're going to use the foundation we have to significantly expand the way we connect capital across the world. We will do more than offer a much broader range of opportunities. We're going to increase our expertise, partnerships, reach, and our assets under management. We are going to turn Investcorp into a truly international financial institution that also helps attract private capital to the six countries of the Gulf Cooperation Council."

What a compelling vision, I thought. Even more striking was that Mohammed spoke of such an ambitious goal in a very humble fashion. Instead of pie in the sky, what he proposed appeared both ambitious and attainable, the result of careful and realistic analyses underpinned by military discipline.

Soon after, I was asked to speak at one of Investcorp's functions, and I began to meet the people who would implement the vision. When I was then invited to join Investcorp's Advisory Board, I was honored and happy to accept more of a front-row seat to an inspiring transformation.

I quickly discovered that other Advisory Board members and many people at Investcorp had the same impression of Mohammed that I did: He is very polite and respectful of people, no matter who they are, and everyone respects and admires him, too. He is a combination of humility and vision, but the steel is clearly there, too. He is an inclusive leader, with the ability to bring together people with a diverse range of backgrounds, talents, and viewpoints and have them function as an organized and disciplined team. By using listening as a strategic skill, he encourages people to be open and honest, even if what they say doesn't match his prior understanding of a situation.

It's not what you normally see on Wall Street.

Over the past few years, Investcorp has expanded its footprint in a very thoughtful manner, through both organic growth and major acquisitions. It's rebranding itself from the Gulf-centered boutique Nemir Kirdar created into a global multi-asset firm with a more diversified client base. That process has been marked by, among other things, the decision to delist from the Bahrain stock market, the enlargement into eight countries—so far—and the expansion into additional asset classes and investor bases. In the eight years since Mohammed became Executive Chairman, Investcorp's assets under management have more than quintupled, from $9 billion to over $50 billion.

As Investcorp continues to grow, its success will, as always, depend on delivering world-class investment performance and client servicing. That's an inherently tricky proposition for any firm to meet in a consistent and durable fashion. That's why the disciplined process Investcorp has followed in its build-out has been and will continue to be so important.

Whether you run a small company or a multinational firm, I believe you always have to ask yourself, "What is my competitive edge?" Especially when compared to some other firms, Investcorp has impressive clarity on this.

It all goes back to the fundamental idea that Investcorp is in the business of building bridges. Originally, those bridges linked the Gulf countries to the rest of the world. Increasingly, though, they're going both ways, introducing the rest of the world to investment opportunities in the fast-growing private markets of the Gulf. And when it comes to doing business there, no firm does it better than Investcorp. In the process, it is helping the region modernize and grow in a more sustainable manner.

It's a cliché to say that the world is constantly changing, but I think it's safe to say that it's a much more uncertain world these days: unusually uncertain. The climate crisis and geopolitical fluidity are just two among many issues that have amplified economic and financial volatility across the globe. When I think about how Investcorp will connect to the future, I always go back to one image: a well-built plane, operated by a clear-headed pilot and assisted by a skilled crew. It's the combination you need to navigate well through turbulent skies.

CHAPTER 1

LEARNING TO FLY

L eading a company like Investcorp has a lot in common with flying a high-performance fighter jet.

I soloed for the first time in a Hawker Hunter fighter jet when I was twenty-two years old and a junior officer in the Royal Air Force of Oman. It wasn't the first time I had been at the controls of a plane; by the time you get to a fighter jet, you've sat in many cockpits and piloted many planes, both with an instructor and on your own. But a fighter jet is something special.

The cockpit is so snug that when you strap into your seat and tighten the safety restraints, you feel as though you're wearing the plane. You're part of the plane and the plane is an extension of you; it responds to the slightest movement of your body. You become a different being: someone sharper, smarter, and more powerful than who you are on earth.

As you brake on the end of the runway, the Rolls-Royce turbojet engine straining for release, equal parts anticipation and fear simmer in your veins. Then the air traffic controller gives you the go-ahead. You shove in the throttle, the engine roars, the G-forces slam you in the chest, and suddenly you're in the air. For one moment, time stops.

In those first moments of flight, your brain is a high-speed computer, taking in massive amounts of data and making split-second decisions.

But in some little corner of your mind, a tiny voice sparkles with astonishment: "I'm doing it. I'm actually doing it!"

/////

That was nearly forty years ago and I've never forgotten that thrill. These days, I "fly a desk" at Investcorp, a multi-billion-dollar global investment firm specializing in alternative asset management. But the excitement and sense of accomplishment—and, yes, the wonder—are familiar. Maybe that's because the characteristics it takes to be a good fighter pilot are the same as those required to run a global investment firm.

You have to be confident. You have to be a good communicator. Whether you're flying by yourself or in formation, everyone needs to know your plan: what the targets are, the order in which the squadron will attack, what to do when things go wrong. Teamwork is essential: you need to know that someone is looking after you and will alert you if an enemy sneaks up behind you. You're constantly honing your situational awareness, so that you carry a clear mental picture of your position in time and space as it relates to the other planes in your squadron, potential attackers, and, of course, the unforgiving ground.

The popular assumption is that both flying and investing satisfy an appetite for risk. I don't think that's quite right. I think they require fortitude in the face of risk. The secret to survival and success is acknowledging the full range of risks and calculating how to mitigate them long before you push the throttle forward or sign off on an action plan.

I became the Executive Chairman of Investcorp in 2015, but looking back, it seems that my whole life prepared me for it.

TURMOIL AND TAKE-OFF

I was born in 1961, in Oman's ancient port city of Sur, located on the eastern tip of the Arabian Peninsula, where the Indian Ocean flows into the Arabian Gulf. My father was a customs official, and when I was eight, he was transferred to Al-Aswad, a small town in the interior of the country near the northern border. It was a desolate patch of desert, but across the road from our house was a small military airstrip where, occasionally, a plane would arrive with supplies for the army.

Oman in the 1960s was a very different country from the Oman of today and the Oman of earlier years. I grew up hearing stories of Oman's proud heritage as the nexus of a sprawling maritime empire that dominated lucrative trade routes throughout the Arabian Gulf, east to India and even China, and all the way down the East African coast to Zanzibar. Ships of all nations rode the monsoon winds to Muscat, bearing gold and pearls from Persia; coffee, tea, and spices from India; coral and ivory from Kenya; and more. Oman's seafaring tradition fostered a cosmopolitan worldview, a truly multicultural mélange of different races and religions.

But those days were ancient history by the time I was born. Oman was much poorer then—oil wouldn't be discovered in commercial quantities until 1964 and exports of oil didn't begin until 1967—and, under the rule of Sultan Said, the country was almost completely isolated from the rest of the world. There was no running water, no electricity, and only six miles of paved road—a single lane stretching from the royal palace to an airstrip—that was used only by the Sultan and the handful of people granted licenses to purchase a car. Radios were banned, as were newspapers, although the vast majority of Omanis couldn't read anyway: in a population of 750,000 people, fewer than 1,000 children were enrolled in school, all of them boys and all limited to primary grades.[1]

We lived a simple life in Al-Aswad, so airplanes seemed like messengers from a different world. You can imagine the magical spell they cast on me. When I heard the engines revving up for take-off, I'd sprint up the stairs to the flat roof of our house and raise my arms to guide the plane into the sky. On especially lucky days, the pilot might fly low enough for my cap to be blown off in the backwash from the single propeller.

At night, I'd lie in bed and imagine myself in the cockpit of one of those Piston Provosts, running through the pre-flight checklist I'd learned about from the pilots whom my father invited to visit: *Hydraulic pressure? Okay. Flight controls? Unlocked. Emergency warnings? None. Full power? On . . .* and then I'd be off, soaring over the windswept sands of the Empty Quarter or swooping and diving like a seabird above the endless blue expanse of the Indian Ocean, the wind whistling over my wings and my heart replete with joy.

Back on earth, I had a happy childhood. The only boy in my family, I was loved and looked after by my parents and my eight sisters. I think that a happy childhood is a great foundation; it allowed me to dream and instilled in me a sense of confidence in the future.

Outside the sunbaked mud-brick walls of our house, though, the future was unstable. Oman was very much a tribal society, and tribes in some regions didn't necessarily want to be united with tribes in other regions. By the mid-1960s, a low-level insurgency in the Dhofar region in the south had spread to the north, and backed by China and the Soviet Union, it flared into a civil war. Rebels attacked any symbol of government, whether it was an army post or a governmental office. Because customs collection was a major source of revenue in Oman's pre-petroleum economy, my father was a target.

One time, a bomb was put under his office chair. By pure chance, he had left his office to inspect a caravan of goods coming in from Dubai when the bomb exploded. It took out his chair and his desk, but he was fine. He was just so lucky.

Another time, I woke up in the middle of the night to strange noises. When I looked out the window, I saw flames licking the walls of the house. We all got out—fast. The next morning, a couple of my sisters and I went to look at the ruins. We found a strange metal object, picked it up, and started playing with it. When our father saw it, he ordered us to leave it alone. It was one of the few times I ever heard him use a stern tone of voice directed at me. Soon after, someone from the Army came to examine the object. I heard him tell my father that it was an anti-personnel land mine. The only reason it hadn't exploded was that the firing pin was crooked.

After that, my father arranged for my mother, sisters, and me to stay with people away from that post.

Looking back, what was so impressive was that my father never showed fear or alarm. He always projected resilience, calm, reassurance, and optimism—traits that would be essential when I took over Investcorp after it had lost its way. "Yes, they bombed my office," he might have said, "but I'm fine. Everything will be all right." He was my first role model as a leader.

In 1970, the year I turned nine, His Majesty Sultan Qaboos bin Said replaced his father on the throne. Educated in the United Kingdom, at Sandhurst, the Royal Military Academy, he jump-started a fundamental transformation of the entire country. For example, knowing the importance of universal education, he didn't wait to build proper schools. Instead, he said, "Let's just provide shade where people can sit, so children can start learning immediately." Classes were held under trees and in tents and in people's homes, with free education for both boys and girls.

Once a year, Sultan Qaboos would tour a different part of the country, visiting all the villages. A tent would be set up, and he would host an audience for the residents, asking them, "What are your issues? How can I help?" The entire cabinet accompanied him to respond.

In the 1960s, Oman was one of the largest sources of expatriate labor in the region, as Omanis who couldn't find work at home hired themselves out to work in the rest of the Gulf region. Within a few years of his accession, Sultan Qaboos embarked on an oil-fueled construction boom, building a modern airport, new schools, hospitals, and hundreds of miles of paved highways. The workers flooded back to help, and as the country began to prosper, they stayed.

It was an exciting time to be in Oman. Everyone was energized and eager to help build our country. To this day, July 23, the date Sultan

Qaboos took power, is celebrated as Renaissance Day, commemorating the start of Oman's rebirth.

In 1971, my father was appointed the head of the State Audit Institution, which was responsible for overseeing the financial dealings of all the government departments. We relocated to the city of Muscat.

As the capital of Oman, Muscat was headquarters for most of the major governmental departments, many of which welcomed teenagers as summer interns. Internships were regarded as a privilege and, to be honest, were open mostly to the privileged. My father would personally talk to a minister or the head of a department and say, "I'd like my son Mohammed to spend some time in your department." That's how I spent my summers from when I was fourteen to when I was seventeen, from 1975 to 1978.

Even though I was a very, very small cog in the wheel of government, I could see how bureaucracy worked and how it could be good or bad, depending on how it was managed. My first internship was in the Customs and Immigration Department. At fourteen, I had no concept of how a ministry was managed or how a government or country was run. I'd deliver a form to be signed by someone in finance or pass along the permission for a shipment to be cleared. I couldn't see why people had to travel for hours from their village to get one signature, then return a few days later for another signature. Always in my mind was the thought, *Why does this require five or six different signatures, instead of just one?*

I learned about teamwork: that teamwork was smart people with specialties in different areas working together for a common goal, that this is ideally how entities function. The reality was often different, though. I couldn't help thinking, *Things should happen quicker, more efficiently.* Bureaucracy could sustain society—or it could stymie and suffocate it.

My last internship was in the Ministry of Oil and Gas. One of the people I learned from was an Egyptian American who was what we would now call the head of communications. He wrote high-level briefs for the minister and the Sultan. We called him "Doctor" because he had earned a Ph.D. He took a particular interest in young people and would explain how to write a good letter or memo, in English and in Arabic. He'd say, "Language is a tool for communication. When people say, 'English is better than Arabic,' they're wrong. It's how you use the language that matters, not the language you use."

A quick aside: My father had me tutored in English, starting from when we moved to Al-Aswad. At the time, the Omani Armed Forces were commanded by British officers. (Oman maintained a close relationship with Great Britain.) My father frequently invited officers to our home; I'd sit at his knee and listen to them talk and would soak up their stories. Knowing English would be a big advantage when I joined the Air Force because everything in the Air Force was conducted in English.

I really enjoyed the internships and I benefited from them, but with each internship it became clearer and clearer to me that I didn't see my future sitting in an office building. I wanted to fly. From the moment I joined the Royal Air Force of Oman at age seventeen, I knew that this was a place I could be part of. I was home.

CALL SIGN: FAHAD ZERO ONE

At first, I just wanted to fly. But after joining the Air Force, I realized that the excitement and speed is in fighter jets. If you don't fly fighters, you're almost a second-class citizen. I immediately thought, *That's what I want to do.*

There was just one problem. My medical test showed a slight curvature of the spine. The Air Force doctors said, "If you fly fighters and have to eject, you will break your spine. We recommend that you don't fly fighters."

I was so upset! But when I had my interview with the Commander of the Air Force, he said, "No, if you qualify to become a fighter pilot, I will let you become a fighter pilot." I guess he was impressed with my determination to fly fighters or die trying. In any case, it was an incentive for me to make sure that I did well.

Oman is a wonderful place to learn to fly. You soar over the aptly named Empty Quarter, where the air is clear and the unbounded desert stretches for miles in every direction. There's almost no habitation, so you can zoom low and buzz saltbushes or dance with the shadow of your plane on the sand dunes. It's the most wonderful three-dimensional playground you can imagine—and we had the best toys. I flew the Hawker Hunter, then the Jaguar (an Anglo-French fighter bomber). My call sign was Fahad Zero One. *Fahad* is the Arabic word for "panther."

Cadets selected for officer training were sent to the U.K's Royal Air Force College in Cranwell. We were billeted with British families to sharpen our English-language skills. It was my first trip outside of Oman, and I was understandably apprehensive.

Before I left, my father gave me the best piece of advice I have ever received. "Of course, they do things differently there," he said. "Some of their customs will seem very strange. My advice is this: Whenever there's anything you don't understand, just ask. Don't judge. Just ask. And they will tell you."

England was a tremendous culture shock. The first surprise was the weather. Where I grew up, the sun shines every day, and you don't need much in the way of warm clothing. By contrast, Lincolnshire, where RAF Cranwell is located, is on the northeast coast of England and is regularly blasted by cold weather coming off the North Sea.

I was assigned to live with a divorced lady with two young daughters. Maybe because I had been brought up with stories about the British Empire, I assumed that the family would be rich and have servants. I arrived at the family's home just before sunset. It was a modest house. I was shown to my room: "This is your bed. Here's the bathroom you'll share with our girls. There's a telephone box down the street where you can call your family. It's next to the bus stop where you'll catch the bus to your college." There were no servants; in fact, I soon realized that this was a family living on the margins. That's why they took in students. But the family was warm and welcoming, and I soon felt at home.

Every day, my misconceptions were challenged and broken. Everything was so strange: people's thinking, their habits, the way they queued for the bus, the way every conversation began with a comment about the weather. But I reminded myself of my father's advice. It was like someone lighting a torch to show me the way. I asked and I kept asking, and gradually I began to understand.

Today, I regularly share my father's advice with young people in the organization: "Don't be too proud to ask questions out of fear that people will laugh at you. You come from a different culture. If they came to your home, there are things they'd want to know. Be willing to ask questions— and keep asking until you understand the answers."

Thanks to my father, I learned to feel comfortable about going into new situations. The unknown, I discovered, was not something to fear but, rather, something to explore with optimism and an open mind.

"IT ALL COMES DOWN TO SITUATIONAL AWARENESS"

Something every fighter pilot learns early on is situational awareness: closely observing your surroundings, picking up cues and analyzing how your decisions could impact the present and future state of affairs. Think of it as risk management in the dimensions of time and space.

Situational awareness depends on good teamwork as much as on good judgment. No matter how good a fighter pilot you are, you simply can't see everything that's going on around you. It's physically impossible to swivel your head while pulling a tight turn and climbing at 715 miles per hour. You need to rely on your wingman and other members of your squadron to guard not just your back but also the entire space in which you're maneuvering.

To be a good team player, you need to be able to learn from your peers, your superiors, and your subordinates. You need to communicate with them—and they need to feel comfortable communicating with you. That means managing your ego: not being afraid to listen to what other people have to say, encouraging people to talk by not filling up the airspace yourself. I call that "confident silence."

Where so many leaders go wrong is that they don't listen. They think they know everything. They don't think they need to develop further. They forget that the pace of change is much faster than we realize, and we can get very rusty *very* quickly.

I had one commander who said to me, "I stopped talking to anybody below the rank of Lieutenant Colonel." When I asked why, he explained, "I saw all those people when I was the regimental commander. I don't need to see them again."

I thought, *That's the biggest mistake you can make.* People on the front lines are often the first to realize that what worked before doesn't quite work anymore, that the rules are changing. They don't always have an easy time explaining it to their higher-ups—or, in a corporate setting, to senior management. The leader is often walled in, in the center of a fortified citadel, and news from the outside has to percolate through layers of people from the periphery where the action is. Consequently, the leader is often the last to know what's really going on—unless he or she builds straightforward communication channels and encourages *everyone* to use them.

I also observed a lot of good leaders. One was Sultan Qaboos. He obsessively tracked down information. He was the head of state, but he had no qualms about showing what he didn't know and no embarrassment about asking questions. If you said, "Let me describe the F-16 and why it should be in our Air Force," he would want to know every detail: "What does that system do? How does this tracking system guide a missile? How is it fired? When it hits the target, what happens?" He never just said, "Okay."

Thanks to similarly diligent leaders, I learned to sharpen my own sense of curiosity. There's no excuse for not doing your homework just because you don't want to ask what might seem like stupid questions. I'd think, *If I need to make a decision and don't have enough information, I'd better get on it myself.*

CHALLENGES AND COMPLICATIONS

While the Dhofar Rebellion ended in 1976, two years before I joined the Air Force, war shakes up military institutions. The British advisors who had been affiliated with the armed forces were now passing the baton to Omani commanders. There were a lot of opportunities for younger people to move up the ranks.

Once you proved yourself as a pilot, the Air Force evaluated your ability to command, and you were given different responsibilities and more training accordingly. There was a well-organized program to identify and sharpen leadership skills. Promotion depended not so much on your years of experience as on your expertise—and you were expected to develop it quickly. First, I commanded a fighter station, then two fighter stations. Then I was put in charge of a region. I didn't stay too long in any one position, just long enough to go through a full cycle of whatever was happening before moving on to the next level.

You were also evaluated on your ability to master the culture of the cockpit. The popular conception of a cocky solo pilot acting on his own initiative literally does not fly. You've been entrusted with a multimillion-dollar piece of equipment deployed on a strategic mission, but you are just one member of the team that enables the mission to be carried out—and every single member of the team is critically important. You quickly learned to be humble and to value teamwork.

It was an exciting time. Between postings, the Air Force sent me to take courses at the Royal Air Force U.K. Staff College, where I earned a Bachelor of Science in Military Science, then to the U.S. National War College and the National Defense University (NDU) in Washington, D.C., which prepares leaders for higher command. The training was fantastic. In addition to students from all the different armed forces, there were people from the CIA, the FBI, and other government agencies. It opened my eyes to different ways of thinking about strategy and partnering with different institutions.

I received my diploma from the NDU in 1992. Ordinarily, the NDU and the National War College would send their evaluations of my work to the Air Force, but to my surprise they insisted on sending it to the Sultan and the Deputy Prime Minister. Soon after, on November 23, 1992, I was appointed Chief of the Royal Air Force of Oman (RAFO). I was thirty-one years old.

That might seem very young, but I was not the only young officer who was given the chance to fill senior leadership positions. It was a time for change and growth, not just in the Air Force but throughout the military. It was also the time to take over from British commanders and put Omanis in the forefront. We all had to step up.

The Air Force I took over was not the Air Force I had joined. My first commander and the man responsible for creating a credible air defense was Erik Bennett, a former British Royal Air Force senior officer who, after being posted to Jordan to help develop its air force, became His Majesty King Hussein's personal pilot. The story goes that when Sultan Qaboos asked the King for advice on setting up Oman's air force, the King immediately replied, "If you want a proper air force, I would recommend Erik."[2] Under Erik's leadership, the RAFO was well trained and well equipped for the time, with strong foundations for continued growth. (He was also a keen naturalist and a passionate protector of the delicate ecosystem of our country.)

Erik retired in 1990 and was succeeded by the RAFO's first Omani commander. Eighteen months later, I was asked to take charge.

When I became the head of the Air Force, my initial mandate, as I saw it, was to raise the standards of the organization to match, if not exceed, its peers. I installed a new set of key performance indicators (KPIs) that were rooted in data. We needed serviceable planes, serviceable weapons, and pilots who knew how to operate them. The training had to be up to the mark, the equipment had to be ready, and all the people involved in maintaining and operating it had to concentrate on one thing: doing their jobs well. My entire focus was on becoming a top fighting unit.

With three commanders in less than three years, many people were suffering from whiplash, especially because the commander I replaced had a different leadership style. I was a known quantity, but I was young both in age and in tenure. I'm sure some people had doubts about this latest leader.

I would have to earn their trust.

Fine-tuning my emotional antenna was another aspect of situational awareness. I had to be sensitive to what were some delicate issues. For example, one of the challenges was that a lot of the people who were now reporting to me had not too long ago been my bosses or trainers. I had to be careful. I wanted to be respectful of their seniority, but at the same time I had to be a leader and push for the change I felt was necessary. There were hundreds of similar issues that needed to be addressed.

I learned that in every instance where you want to instigate change there will be three types of people: those who embrace it, those who are on the fence, and those who reject it. You can work with the first type and you can persuade the second. But for those who reject it completely, at a certain point, you'll have to say, with respect, "Thank you for your service. Maybe this is no longer for you."

MAINTAINING A "CONFIDENT SILENCE"

Another challenge I faced was combining military responsibilities with political responsibilities. As the commander of the Air Force, I reported directly to the Sultan, so my headquarters was also the center of the Air Force's political operations.

The expectations for military responsibility are straightforward. First and foremost is performance. The Air Force is data driven, and your performance—whether you're a pilot or a mechanic, whether you're leading a squadron or commanding the entire Air Force—is constantly measured and assessed against a series of benchmarks. Mediocrity is simply not tolerated.

Politics was an entirely different matter. For me, it was like flying into a cloud without instruments. Listening to people spout a lot of rubbish and being expected to agree was a skill I didn't have.

I was so young—remember, I took command of the Air Force when I was just thirty-one—and, in my view, I was surrounded by dinosaurs. What I had to learn was that even though some of them had gone extinct, they still had the power to damage you if they thought you ignored them or didn't show them proper respect.

One of my former commanders and mentors saw that I was floundering. He said, "The general who is now the chairman of the armed forces is your boss, no matter what you think about him. You have to salute him and show respect, not just because of his position but—and this is the most important thing—because the damage he can do to you and the Air Force is not worth your *not* observing these niceties."

Of course, he was right. Honing political skills was just a different kind of situational awareness.

I listened to his advice—and that of others whom I respected—and I tried to apply it. But it really wasn't in my nature to be good at politics. The best I could do was learn to keep my mouth shut and maintain a "confident silence."

Sometimes the "confident silence" was less about projecting quiet assurance and more about clamping my mouth shut to prevent any airing of my frustration. But the result was that I learned to keep a straight face and listen—and absorb and absorb. By allowing people the freedom to run on, I could sit back and identify any useful nuggets.

I began to see that less could be more. Because it was futile—or worse—to attack these dinosaurs in public, I began to see the power in indirect leadership. I learned that while confronting people in the public forum may seem like the most efficient way to address issues, in reality it's more effective to sort things out on the side, in private—to take a soft approach, to persuade rather than command.

People often act differently when there's an audience. They may bluster or go on the attack, so they don't lose the respect of their colleagues. The key is for you to dial down the emotions before they go into the danger zone. Find another forum and make it a conversation, rather than a confrontation. When you take the trouble to speak to people individually and in private, they will say exactly what they feel. That's another kind of situational awareness. It's another way to gather the data you need to make an informed decision.

And sometimes I had to acknowledge the value in a strategic retreat or look for small wins rather than large victories. For example, we had to maintain connections with other countries, which we did by sending our people to embed in their air force. They'd come back without much return on our investment of time and money. But there wasn't much we could do about it. We had to have that relationship, and that gesture was the cost of doing business. The best we could do was try not to let these guys fail, either when they were away or when they came back and had to catch up. It wasn't their fault that they were used as the "glue" in country-to-country politics.

The ultimate lesson, as my former commander pointed out, is that even though you think—and you may be right—that taking a meeting with someone who doesn't add value is a waste of time, *not* taking that meeting can cause more problems later.

I wish I had learned that lesson earlier. In my defense, I'll just say that this kind of indirect leadership is so quiet and unassuming that it's easy to overlook. You have to deliberately search for it in order to see it. Ironically, my desire to be straightforward and no-nonsense complicated things for me and made it more difficult to achieve my goal of improving the Air Force as quickly as I would have liked.

FIGHTING FOR THE FALCON

In the end, the whole process of bringing the Air Force back to where we had been under Erik Bennett's leadership took two to three years. But I believed we could be even better.

I wanted us to fly the F-16.

The Fighting Falcon set the standard by which every other fighter jet in the world is judged. It's fast, effective, and reliable, highly maneuverable, and adaptable to a variety of roles, from air defense to ground attacks. It combines a brilliant weapons system with a powerful engine in a single-seat plane, so it doesn't require many people to operate it—which is perfect for a small air force like ours. It's relatively low cost compared to any of its peers. And it connected us with the U.S. Air Force and its intelligence, experience, and logistics for the long term.

There was one hitch, however, and it was a major one: up to that point, all our fighters were British. (The Jaguar was an Anglo-French collaboration, and anyway, it was several decades older than the F-16; while it's a great fighter-bomber, it's not as powerful or maneuverable as the F-16.) Switching planes would require switching long-established supply chains whose contracts were a key part of military budgets—not just ours but also those of the governments whose defense manufacturers designed, built, and serviced the planes. In other words, this wasn't just a military or economic decision. It was a crucial political one.

Fortunately, the five other member nations in the GCC—the Gulf Cooperation Council, which comprises Bahrain, Kuwait, Oman, Qatar, Saudi Arabia, and the United Arab Emirates—all had really strong air forces with advanced equipment. After one of our joint exercises, the Sultan wanted to know how things went.

"Look, Your Majesty," I said, "the Saudis have the F-15. The Bahrainis and the UAE have the F-16. The Kuwaitis have the F-18. We have the Hawk"—a light fighter. "We did what we could, but we had no chance against them."

The Sultan asked, "What shall we do?"

I said, "To be able to participate on a par with those forces, we cannot have a Land Rover go up against a tank." (The Sultan was an army man, so he understood the comparison.) "We need a better fighter."

I used to invite the Sultan to visit the Royal Air Force of Oman once a year. We would host him by himself—no ministers, no government representatives, just the pilots and other officers. He would ask them questions and vice versa, and they'd talk together face to face. That sowed the seed of mutual trust: he knew he was getting honest opinions, without any sugarcoating.

So when I said, "We need a better fighter," he agreed that what we had wasn't good enough.

That started a series of studies and comparisons and due diligence. And extra training. Everyone realized that they needed to seriously upgrade their skills to fly the F-16. Being an F-16 fighter pilot was something worth fighting for. It didn't just boost their skills; it skyrocketed morale.

WHAT MAKES A GOOD LEADER

As I climbed the ranks in the Air Force, I learned a lot about leadership: what being a good leader entails and where so many leaders go wrong. The skills that make a good fighter pilot are not necessarily the same that produce a good leader. I observed my colleagues and superior officers to determine what they did well and where they came up short.

In every leadership position, pushing for better performance and growth can sort out a lot of problems. People want to be part of something that is bigger than what they can achieve on their own. That's why you want someone who can come in with a vision, devise a strategy, and build a team that can execute it. My vision for the Air Force was to build an organization good enough to fly the best fighter planes in the world. Later, my vision for Investcorp was to take a company managing $10 billion of AUM (assets under management) and triple its size in five years or less. (Whenever I refer to Investcorp's AUM in this book, it also includes assets managed by third-party managers on Investcorp's behalf.) In both cases, I had faith that people could not only achieve our goals but also achieve something even more valuable: confidence in their ability to exceed their own expectations.

Equally important for good leadership is *how* you push for better performance. Some leaders feel they have to be aggressive, by shouting or bullying or being unnecessarily hard on people. I don't agree with that. I believe leaders should empower their people to achieve their goals: empower them to be creative, remove the blockages in their way, get them excited about doing the right thing. You can raise the targets and make sure people follow the plan, but you don't have to destroy their ego or their self-esteem.

When you push for better performance, you have to be humble: let your people know that they can communicate with you, that you're approachable, that you're a human being like them. Those ideas go hand-in-hand.

I've seen so many people do this well, starting with my father. He lived in dangerous places in dangerous times, but he never missed an opportunity to reach out to people at all levels, whether it was his deputy or "just" a security guard.

I, too, tried to be a role model. Your people should never say, "But you don't do what you're asking us to do." Fortunately, I had continued to fly fighter jets as I moved up in command. In the Air Force, the more types of planes you fly, the more credibility you have. I flew two different planes—the Jaguar and the Hawker Hunter—so even though I no longer spent as much time in the cockpit when I took command of the Air Force, those reporting to me could say, "He knows what he's doing."

Knowledge is power. In the Air Force, the mere act of getting out of the office, leaving behind the meetings and papers, to walk down the flight line and actually fly a plane, that's not just an empty gesture, it's also a valuable investment of your time.

Why? Because it enhances your situational awareness.

I used to spend two days of the week visiting air force bases. Whenever possible, I liked to fly, because when you fly, you talk to the entire chain: the pilots and engineers and ground crews. When you're at your desk at headquarters, you may be asking yourself, *Why isn't this thing working? Why is that delayed?* You get the answers you really need when you get out on the tarmac.

Talking to the people on the tarmac provides raw data you couldn't get any other way. What's the condition of the planes? Are they prepared for action? Do the maintenance crews have the necessary tools and training? Do they work as an efficient team?

When you go to the squadron ready room to get briefed on your flight, you get another set of inputs from the flight-safety people who are sorting out your kit and the pilots who will go up with you. Simple questions—How is this helmet working out? Is it entirely new or just an upgraded version? How long have the oxygen masks been delayed? What restrictions are being imposed?—lead to other questions, which sharpen your perspective.

After the briefing, you go out to the airplane. There's the engineer who prepared it and the technician who signed off on it. You ask them: "What have you been doing this week?" "How have things been this month?" "What did you learn from that exercise your team participated in?"

When people see that you're trying to take part in what they do, they'll talk. Many commanders don't like that interaction. Fighter pilots, especially, are not shy. You go to a crew room, and they really charge at you: "Why isn't that missile working?" "Why isn't that fuse sparking?" "Why did the upgrade get delayed?"

I always liked doing this because I could see first-hand what the problems were, even if I didn't have good answers. It was all part of gathering and processing evidence, and then distilling out the most valuable findings. And it was a great way to sense the morale of the organization.

These inputs are crucial because you need to center your situational awareness in an organization before you can implement meaningful change. As the saying goes, If you don't know where you are, how will you get to where you want to be?

I followed the same precepts when I took over at Investcorp. I travel a lot: we have fourteen offices around the globe, and I try to visit each one at least twice a year. I try to talk to everyone: our employees, from the most junior associates to managing directors; our clients; and our industry peers. That's how I take the pulse of the organization and how I evaluate where we stand in comparison to others. That's how to articulate the direction we need to go and how to identify the roadblocks that prevent us from getting there.

What people don't realize about fighter pilots is not only that we're probably more thoughtful than the popular conception of just being adrenaline junkies, but also that we're incredibly disciplined. We have to be. You have to study your mission and make sure you have everything required to do the job, and be able to return safely to your base. You have to check your airplane and its systems and weapons. Once you're in the air, you have to keep looking around to ensure that your instruments are giving you the correct information, that your wingmen are fine, and that you know where you are in the sky.

The discipline comes from honing your reflexes flight after flight, day after day, so you get better and better. That's the discipline most people don't see.

The drill is familiar to anyone who is a high achiever, man or woman, no matter what their career, whether they're a fighter pilot or an investment manager. We're data driven. We have to be, because all those data points provide the context for our decisions. They define our place on the map in relation to where we've been, where we're going, and where we need to be: our overall situational awareness.

That's why I don't accept comparing yourself to people or organizations that are doing something similar to what you're doing. That's not going to help you become the best you can be. From the moment I took command of the Royal Air Force of Oman, I focused on upgrading our entire system. Similarly, from my first day as Executive Chairman of Investcorp, I compared us to the most successful players in the field globally. We were a fraction of their size. But once you start measuring yourself against the top benchmarks, you start thinking about how they think and analyzing how they achieved their success. Once you put yourself in that frame of mind, you can't help but improve *everything*. From then on, it's just a matter of having the discipline to follow through, day after day, week after week, and year after year.

That's how leaders can inspire their people to be better than they ever believed, to reach for targets they never thought they could hit. That's how you build a bridge to the future.

A NEW DIRECTION

I held the post of the chief of the Air Force for ten years. The usual tenure was four years. It was a great job, and I probably could have stayed another ten years, but I was only forty-two. It was time to move on.

The question was, What should I do next?

I had no plans. I just wanted to learn something new.

Back in 1992, when I was at the National Defense University, I had learned about a program on national and international security at the John F. Kennedy School of Government, at Harvard University. The NDU recommended I attend. The Air Force gave me permission, and I went. I loved it. I loved seeing so much intellectual firepower in one place and having so many options to learn. I promised myself, *If I get the chance, I'll come here and do a proper degree.*

Now, eleven years later, the chance was here.

I enrolled in the program for a master's degree in public administration. The nice thing about the public administration program at Harvard is that it covers an enormous number of subjects. You can take courses at the business school, the law school, even at other schools, like the Massachusetts Institute of Technology. I dived right in.

Every class taught me something new. One of the classes I particularly loved was on negotiations. In the Air Force, I had been involved in high-level negotiations with the U.S. government—for example, to hammer out access agreements and renewals. To actually sit in a class and analyze the science behind strategic conversations was fantastic. Another class that seemed tailored specifically to me was on managing global financial institutions. The professor brought in guest speakers from JP Morgan, Fannie Mae, Freddie Mac, and BlackRock, the world's largest asset manager.

I had no idea where this was going to lead. I just loved learning and, especially, learning in this environment. The program mixed people of all ages—the youngest participant was twenty-five and the oldest was in his early seventies. It was so much fun being with such smart people from different backgrounds and with different perspectives.

I was, perhaps, naïve in not realizing that people go to the Kennedy School as much for the contacts as for the subject matter. Later, I would discover that a newly minted Harvard degree would open many doors and give me added credibility. (For example, when I first met Nemir Kirdar, the founder of Investcorp, he said that it meant so much to him that a fellow Arab had not only become the Commander of the Royal Air Force of Oman but when I retired—our commission in the RAFO is for life and only the Sultan can grant permission to leave the service—and, rather than rest on my laurels, I became a student at Harvard.) I honestly did not foresee that. But it was proof of what I often told my children: if you do the right things, success will find you.

Meanwhile, the program helped me clarify what I wanted to do next: something in finance and business. The Kennedy School had shown me a world I hadn't known before, and it introduced me to some of the smartest people in that world, who intended to leverage their competence and confidence to effect change in an even wider sphere.

I knew I was ready for a challenge, and I knew that the challenge would be leading an organization. I wasn't looking for nitty-gritty work. I was interested in strategy, not tactics. I wanted to take something from here to there, to make it grow.

I had done that as the Commander of the Royal Air Force of Oman. I was proud of improving and upgrading our system of leadership training and development, of facilitating a path for women in the Air Force (Oman is one of the few Arab countries whose military accepts women), and of convincing the leadership to shift its fighter jet platform to the F-16.

The world of finance and business would be different from the military, but I believed—and still do—that the leadership skills would be the same. Once you know how to lead people or organizations, it's just a matter of getting acclimatized to different systems and tools. It's like moving from one airplane to another: you need to learn a new cockpit and checklist, but you already have the aptitude and the mindset. The flying is the same.

After getting my degree from the Kennedy School, I returned to Oman and cofounded Rimal Investment Projects, an investment firm that connected high-net-worth investors with entrepreneurs, initially in Oman and eventually throughout the Gulf. It was another way for me to help my country grow.

Then, in 2007, I was introduced to Nemir Kirdar, the founder of Investcorp.

One of my friends from the military was Field Marshal Peter Inge, the former Chief of the General Staff for the British Army, then the Chief of the Defence Staff (the British equivalent of being the chairman of the Joint Chiefs of Staff in the U.S.). Peter was on the Investcorp Advisory Board when he asked me help facilitate a meeting among Sultan Qaboos, His Highness the Crown Prince of Abu Dhabi (now President) Sheikh Mohamed Bin Zayed Al Nahyan, and His Majesty King Abdullah of Jordan at Nemir's house in the South of France.

"Why would these heads of state want to go to Nemir's house?" I asked Peter. "They're already close to each other. They can schedule their own visits." Peter responded, "Why don't you ask Nemir what he wants? He's in London," as was I. A mutual friend from the Arabian Gulf made the connection.

When I contacted Nemir, he was upset with Peter. He felt there had been a misunderstanding. He knew that all these leaders were acquainted with each other and didn't need an intermediary, he explained. What he meant was that if these people were in the French Riviera in the summer—which they often were—he would be honored to host them over lunch at his home for a strategic discussion about politics and investments.

Once we sorted out the misunderstanding, I told him I would be happy to make the overture to those leaders. Then Nemir asked if I was staying in London for a while. When I said yes, he invited me to lunch.

We met at Investcorp's office at 48 Grosvenor Street, a short walk from Hyde Park, in the elegant Mayfair district. It's an impressive building and the office matched its surroundings, with polished wood, glowing oriental carpets, and fine art prints on the walls. Nemir wasn't particularly tall, but his personality was so immense and magnetic that I was immediately drawn to him.

At the time, I knew very little about Investcorp, other than the fact that it was a Bahrain-based investment firm that had owned such high-profile brands as Tiffany, Gucci, and Saks Fifth Avenue. Investcorp had just celebrated its twenty-fifth anniversary, so it made sense for me to ask Nemir about what he envisioned for the firm's future.

To my surprise, he said that he wanted out. "Look, I built this organization from scratch," he said. "I created a bridge for wealthy people from the Gulf to invest in the West. To get to the next level, we need sovereign wealth funds and governments in the Gulf to use Investcorp as their investment vehicle, to protect it and help it grow. But I've done my bit. I've had enough and I'm ready to leave."

Then he said, "Would you like to be associated with Investcorp?"

I asked him what he meant by "associated." He said, "Would you like to join the Board of Directors?"

I liked Nemir right off the bat on a personal level. I was also impressed with what he had achieved in his career. In twenty-five years, he had built a $10 billion firm from nothing. I felt he was someone I could learn from, someone I'd like to be associated with. The initial attraction for me was Nemir, before the firm.

I asked for a few days to think about his offer. During that time, I asked around and did my own research. Everything I heard sounded good.

I called Nemir and said, "I'm willing to serve on Investcorp's board."

CHAPTER 2

THE FOUNDER'S CURSE

When I joined Investcorp's Board of Directors in the spring of 2008, the firm had just celebrated its twenty-fifth anniversary and its best year ever.

It was a golden time for Investcorp. "There was an aura of glamor about Investcorp," recalled Rishi Kapoor, who left Citibank to join our finance department in 1992 and has been our co-CEO since 2015. "It was the antithesis of Citi. It was small and nimble, free of the bureaucratic burden typical of very large organizations. Its people seemed to have found the right balance between being seasoned and being entrepreneurial. The firm was headquartered in Bahrain but had a meaningful presence in North America and Europe. And it was doing something that at that time was truly unique, which was making private equity and real estate investments and syndicating them to high-net-worth families in the Gulf. None of us were aware of any bank or financial services firm at that time that did that."

Investcorp's glamorous reputation was matched by its investments in luxury brands: Tiffany, Gucci, Saks Fifth Avenue, French jeweler Chaumet, Swiss watchmaker Breguet, and other high-end names. Investcorp, Rishi said, "cast a spell."

Hazem Ben-Gacem was similarly enthralled when he joined the firm two years later, in 1994. He told me, "I walked into the lobby and my impression was, 'Wow, this is elegant.' Nemir Kirdar had a lot of gravitas. He oozed dignity. Marry that with what I heard about successful transactions like the Tiffany IPO and audacious deals like acquiring Saks for $1.5 billion—a huge amount in 1990—and I thought, 'I want to be a part of that.'" (Today, Hazem is Investcorp's other co-CEO.)

THE INCEPTION OF INVESTCORP

Nemir Kirdar had emigrated from Iraq to the United States in 1958, in the wake of a violent coup by anti-Western military leaders. Then twenty-two, he finished his undergraduate degree in economics and took an entry-level position as a teller at a regional bank in Arizona. From there, he climbed to overseeing Chase Manhattan's Middle East operations, based out of Bahrain. His role model was Chase chairman David Rockefeller. In addition to being a businessman of outstanding international stature, Rockefeller was a visionary statesman with an unparalleled network of contacts.

A little bit of background: In October 1973, a year before Nemir joined Chase, the Organization of the Petroleum Exporting Countries (OPEC) announced an oil embargo targeting those countries that supported Israel during the Yom Kippur War. The resulting oil crisis sent oil prices skyrocketing: By the end of the embargo, in January 1974, the price per barrel had nearly quadrupled, from just below US$3 per barrel to nearly $12 per barrel globally, with prices significantly higher in the United States.[1]

The result was an unprecedented accumulation of wealth in OPEC member nations. Every financial institution around the globe wanted a piece of the pie, including Chase. Nemir was appointed to launch Chase Manhattan's operations in the Arabian Gulf.

Banks at the time offered only conventional outlets for investment: bank deposits, marketable securities in stocks and bonds, and certain direct investments, such as buying a hotel or a shopping center. With so much wealth in the Gulf, Nemir saw first-hand the potential for something new: a specialized financial institution that operated on both sides of the

Atlantic and offered investments in nontraditional , i.e., alternative lines of business, like privately owned companies and real estate. As he wrote in his memoir, *Need. Respect. Trust,* "Why not build a bridge between the opportunities in the West and the surplus funds in the Gulf?"[2]

The governments in the Gulf countries had already created state-owned sovereign wealth funds to channel their extra oil monies. However, sovereign wealth funds at that time were not the massive investment vehicles they are today. They were much smaller, mainly because the governments initially channeled the oil revenues into their countries' infrastructure, building highways, housing, airports, hospitals, the electrical grid, desalination plants, and, of course, the petroleum industry. There wasn't a lot of surplus. Only after those basic needs had been attended to were significant amounts of money pumped into sovereign wealth funds.

Furthermore, that money tended to be managed very conservatively. Most of the funds invested primarily in liquid securities as an extension of the central banks: global public equities, fixed-income instruments, and prime real estate opportunities. And, as with pension funds worldwide, these official entities preferred to deal with long-established financial institutions in New York, London, Frankfurt, or Tokyo that boasted decades-long track records and traditional blue-chip investments.

Private equity was still a fairly new concept in the West. With the exception of Abu Dhabi's ADIA and Kuwait's KIA, which were among the oldest and most sophisticated wealth funds, private equity deals simply weren't part of the sovereign wealth fund investment landscape.

Nemir focused instead on the burgeoning private sector; that's where the money was for what he had in mind. Thanks to the enormous amounts being poured into infrastructure in the Gulf, the private sector was growing richer and richer by doing the actual construction and providing the necessary products and services.

"Soon the private sector's income would exceed its expenses," Nemir wrote, "and then it too would need to invest its accumulating surplus funds. But this emerging and fast-growing private sector would probably not have the same access to the world's most established organizations as the government money managers did. Nor would these individuals get the same attention from them. Moreover, there were local cultural habits and behaviors that would influence the preference of these private individuals in investing their funds."[3]

He saw an opportunity. Investcorp was founded in 1982.

The firm would be headquartered in Manama, the capital of the Kingdom of Bahrain. Widely acknowledged as the financial capital of the region, Bahrain offered a respected regulatory environment and a wide talent pool. In addition, its central location meant that it was less than an hour's flight from all the countries in the Gulf.

Nemir envisioned an institution formed and capitalized by Gulf shareholders to serve the needs of Gulf investors: a boutique firm offering mid-market (between $250 million and $1 billion) investment opportunities in North America and Western Europe to the rapidly growing class of increasingly wealthy individuals in the Gulf. At the time, the developed markets of North America and Europe accounted for close to three-quarters of the world's GDP. Their governments followed the rule of law, and their financial markets were both sophisticated and liquid: investors had many options for where they could put their money, and they could buy and sell their holdings easily. Within those markets, Investcorp focused on two asset classes: private equity and real estate. (Hedge funds were added in 1996.)

Few individual investors at the time were familiar with alternative asset management—a term that includes investing in privately owned companies, as opposed to buying shares offered on the public securities markets. Today, private equity is an acknowledged asset class. Back then, Investcorp was one of the very early entrants.

THE DEAL-BY-DEAL MODEL

Investcorp's formula for success was the deal-by-deal model. Investcorp would identify a promising acquisition—usually a family-owned firm that the heirs weren't interested in running, or a founder-led company whose leader either wanted additional funds and management expertise to take them to the next level or was ready to cash out.

"Corporate orphans" were another crop of low-hanging fruit. During the conglomerate boom of the 1960s and 1970s, large corporations diversified their holdings with unrelated acquisitions that seemed like a good idea at the time: A classic example was ITT, an American manufacturing company specializing in components for the aerospace, transportation, and energy markets, buying Sheraton Hotels and Resorts. These non-core businesses didn't receive the management attention and financial support they needed to thrive, so when there was a change in leadership or the market, the parent company would put the "orphan" on the block, often at a discounted price. That's how Investcorp snapped up Tiffany's. The luxury jewelry firm had been acquired by Avon, a mass-market cosmetics company, in 1978; it was put up for sale five years later.

Investcorp would buy companies with its working capital, which was a pool of liquidity kept available to make the acquisitions that it would underwrite—what we call "using our balance sheet." Investcorp then syndicated the deal—that is, it invited client-investors to participate in buying the company. However, because it was important for Investcorp to be aligned with its clients, the firm always kept a small part of its balance sheet invested in the acquisition. It was Investcorp's way of having skin in the game.

Investcorp's clients would take on the ownership rights—and the risk—of the acquired company, while Investcorp retained control over the investment and the company's management team. The idea was that Investcorp would improve its operations, boost its bottom line, and after three to five years, bring it to the public market through an IPO or sell it on the private market, preferably at a higher price. That's what happened with Tiffany's: Investcorp bought it in 1984, restored its lost luster, and less than three years later, sold it in a public offering that recouped more than ten times its initial investment.

As Investcorp grew and prospered, the shareholders, who had committed the original equity to create the firm, were paid small dividends and the remaining profits were used to further bolster the balance sheet. While the equity capital initially supported a small liquidity pool used to underwrite Investcorp's first acquisitions, with the growth in the value of the original equity, Investcorp was able to expand the size of its balance sheet, and so too its available working capital. This enabled the firm to buy larger and larger companies, culminating in a massive deal only eight years after its founding: the 1990 acquisition of Saks Fifth Avenue for $1.5 billion.

The deal-by-deal formula was Investcorp's differentiator. That it worked so well demonstrated Nemir's knowledge of his clientele and, even more important, their trust in him. Each deal was a building block in a relationship. There were plenty of other professionals—some of them hucksters, some completely legitimate—trying to tap the wealth in the Gulf. But Nemir understood his clients deeply. He knew how they liked to invest and what they liked to invest in. He knew how they liked to be treated. He literally spoke their language.

"We would go to the clients individually and present each transaction as a unique investment opportunity," recalled Savio Tung, who joined the firm two years after it was founded and served as its Chief Investment Officer before retiring after thirty-two years. (He is still affiliated with Investcorp as a Senior Advisor.) "They could pass but they knew that some other investor might come in. If they didn't grab the chance, they might lose it. Our investors in the Gulf liked that. They liked to think they could exercise their judgment to cherry-pick and we gave them that accommodation."

However, the deal-by-deal model was a double-edged sword.

Its intrinsic weakness was that it didn't allow for long-term committed capital. Other firms asked investors to contribute to a "blind pool," a fund which was invested at the firm's discretion, and to commit to leaving their money in that fund for a certain period of time, usually ten years. That money was literally a firm's nest egg. Investcorp often held on to companies in its portfolio even when they weren't doing well initially, nursing them along until they became profitable. If you have a large pool of capital to draw upon through a fund vehicle, you can feed it into the ailing company while continuing to make other investments or payouts to investors. Not having committed capital limited Investcorp's flexibility.

The deal-by-deal model also limited the field of potential investors. It didn't meet the needs of institutional investors. The challenge of attracting institutional investors is described in more detail in chapter 8, but basically, large institutions don't have the time, the patience, or the personnel to evaluate lots of individual deals. They prefer to invest in blind pool funds, overseen by a team of managers with a stellar track record. Investcorp's decision to eschew funds also meant eschewing the large infusions of committed capital from institutional investors, which further limited the organization's flexibility.

Nemir understood Investcorp's clients through and through. Funds in blind pool funds may have mitigated the risk for investors, but they dampened the thrill of having a big stake pay off. Funds were also less personal—and Investcorp was founded on personal relationships.

Consequently, Investcorp asked its investors for neither a blind-pool contribution nor a time commitment. This meant that while everyone shared in the rewards, Investcorp carried much of the risk. And because the deal-by-deal model was the main source of revenue for the firm, it represented an especially high level of risk.

CRUMBLING FOUNDATIONS

How much risk was involved became evident barely six months after I became a member of Investcorp's Board of Directors. On September 15, 2008, Lehman Brothers collapsed, setting off the worst financial crisis since the Great Depression of the 1930s. The equity markets had started to sell off even before the Lehman debacle, and they continued plummeting for the next year and a half. When the mortgage bubble burst, real estate portfolios were decimated. The banking system was on the verge of imploding. In the United States, Americans lost $9.8 trillion in wealth as their home values and savings vaporized. Economists later calculated that more than $2 trillion in global economic growth was lost, a drop of nearly 4 percent between the pre-recession peak in the second quarter of 2008 and the first quarter of 2009.[4]

In July 2007, barely twelve months earlier, Investcorp had marked its twenty-fifth anniversary, topping off three of its best years ever with a blow-out year. (Investcorp reports its earnings according to a fiscal year ending on June 30.) Its return on many investments was a jaw-dropping five to ten times—an astonishing performance given that the firm had held many of its investments for just three years. When the fiscal year closed in June 2008, Investcorp counted about $12 billion in assets under management (AUM): $8 billion in client money and $4 billion in Investcorp's own capital, of which $1.25 billion was in the form of equity and the remainder in loans.

The firm's business model at that time was based on three pillars: private equity, real estate, and hedge funds. As the world plunged into what would become known as the global financial crisis, two of those pillars were crumbling.

Hedge funds have a reputation for being so complicated that only sophisticated investors can understand them. In fact, they're based on a simple concept: by buying assets that are expected to rise in value *as well as* shorting assets whose prices are expected to decrease, fund managers can "hedge" their bets against market vagaries and come out ahead. Of course, hedge funds *did* become complicated as fund managers spiced up their strategies to get exposure to a broad range of asset classes and investment styles: macro, arbitrage, activism, distressed investments, options, futures, and so on. But the basic idea held true, and by the 1990s, the sector really began to boom, attracting both mainstream investors and institutional investors such as pension funds, insurance companies, and sovereign wealth funds—and Investcorp.

What appealed to Investcorp was that hedge fund managers typically invested their own money in their funds. That synced with the firm's own philosophy of maintaining a financial stake in its business. Coming off the wildly profitable sale of its stake in Gucci in 1995 and 1996, Investcorp had almost too much cash on hand. That liquidity needed to be diversified and put to work.

Investcorp initially deployed its own money into hedge funds. When it liked the returns the hedge funds were generating, in 1996 it launched its own hedge fund platform to provide clients with a broader array of investment opportunities. Everyone benefited. In fact, the main driver of Investcorp's record profits in 2007 was the return from hedge funds.

"I remember in early 2008, a number of senior people warning that, purely from an exposure point of view, we had too much money in hedge funds," recalled Investcorp veteran and now Senior Advisor Tim Mattar. But the funds were doing so well that reducing exposure was a difficult decision.

By 2008, Investcorp had invested about $2.2 billion of its capital in hedge funds—close to *two times* the size of its equity base in one asset class.

Then there was the real estate platform. Investcorp's Core Plus strategy involved buying properties that were in good, but maybe not great, locations, with high-quality tenants and reliable occupancy rates. Typical Core Plus investments might include residential housing, warehouses, and manufacturing facilities—properties producing a reliable cash flow that can be bumped up through light improvements, management efficiencies, or increasing the quality of the tenants. "Core Plus" is synonymous with "growth and income" equity investing: a low-to-moderate risk that throws off between 8 and 10 percent returns annually. (The firm's present real estate strategy is described in more detail in chapter 6.)

But not every investor was satisfied with a slow-and-steady approach of mid-single-digit cash yields and a small capital gain. (Yes, in those days, 8 to 10 percent returns were considered slow and steady.) Some clients wanted the 17 to 20 percent returns that came from exposure to high-risk, high-reward development projects.

While continuing to keep one foot firmly planted in Core Plus, Investcorp began to explore development deals: the Desert Passage shopping mall attached to the Aladdin Hotel on the Las Vegas Strip, a housing development called Las Vegas Lakes, a number of golf courses, then a portfolio of full-service hotels in the southeastern and midwestern United States. The deals grew bigger and bigger, as did the profits.

"By the end of 2006, we said, 'This real estate market is looking a bit frothy. We're going to scale down in 2007,'" Tim Mattar recalled. "That's what we did. We stepped back, sold a lot of stuff, and significantly reduced our exposure. We then sat there for 12 months while the market continued to move up. So at the end of 2007, beginning of 2008, we increased our real estate exposure."

In early 2008, the firm closed on an office building in Midtown Manhattan. And not just any office building: 280 Park Avenue was a trophy building at a trophy address at 48th Street and Park Avenue, right in the sweet spot of the exclusive Park Avenue business corridor. Its two towers were leased to thirty-seven high-profile finance companies, including Deutsche Bank, Credit Suisse First Boston, GE Capital—and Investcorp.[5] The National Football League (NFL) had its headquarters there. The deal was theoretically Core Plus, but it was so leveraged that it wouldn't throw off any cash for two years.

Almost nine months to the day after closing on 280 Park Avenue, Lehman Brothers crashed, sending a seismic shock through the global financial industry and shattering two of Investcorp's three foundational pillars.

The hedge funds cratered. The hedge fund industry as a whole dropped by 22 percent; Investcorp lost 20 percent. Twenty percent of $2.2 billion in holdings is $440 million—a gut-wrenching blow.

And that wasn't all.

The bottom fell out of the real estate market, as well. Deutsche Bank gave up their space at 280 Park Avenue. The NFL left and other tenants also pulled out. The value of the building plummeted; the equity was gone. There were no tenants to lease the space and no cash flow to satisfy the debt. Other properties also stopped generating revenue, as people could no longer afford to buy homes or stay in hotels. Investcorp's real estate AUM went to almost zero.

There were further losses in the private equity investments.

What was so shocking, Tim later told me, was how fast everything fell apart. "This was not a gradual unspooling," he said. "It was like a tidal wave. Everyone was glued to their Bloomberg terminals and television screens, watching Lehman employees carrying boxes of their belongings out of the building, with a sick feeling in our stomachs. We didn't know what was hidden in other banks' balance sheets. If a 150-year-old institution like Lehman could be wiped out, who would be next?"

Almost overnight, Investcorp lost nearly $800 million. More than half the firm's total equity was wiped out.

The future looked grim.

Just a few months earlier, Nemir Kirdar had been on the verge of a triumphant retirement. Now, he was flying around the Gulf, desperately seeking capital to shore up the firm's tottering balance sheet. And the investors he expected to lend a helping hand were giving him the cold shoulder. Over and over again, he was dismissed with the comment, "These are tough times for us, too" or he was told, "We'll get back to you"—and then never heard back. The congenial face-to-face meetings he was accustomed to had given way to an impersonal "Send your team."

Although investors in Investcorp company shares held steady, there were painful defections among clients who had invested in Investcorp portfolio products. Some of them even demanded that Investcorp return their money because they thought the firm was going bankrupt.

It was a terrible blow to Nemir. The firm had been built on personal relationships, and now his twenty-five-year investment in those relationships had evaporated. He took the lack of support personally. We would have dinner together and he would say, over and over, "They forget who I am, they forget what I did for them."

It was touch and go, but Nemir eventually scraped together $500 million of preferred equity, a class of stock that takes precedence over common stock in the payment of dividends and the liquidation of assets. In Investcorp's case, preferred shareholders received a 12 percent dividend per year for the first five years, after which Investcorp had the right to redeem the shares—if it could afford to. It was a high price to pay, but the company didn't have a choice.

Daniel Lopez-Cruz, who at the time headed up Investcorp's European private equity line of business, told me, "Without that $500 million of preferred equity that Nemir almost single-handedly raised, I very much doubt that we would have survived." Daniel is an even-tempered guy, not prone to hyperbole. But looking back, he recalled, "It was a near-death experience."

The ship didn't sink, but it was gravely damaged. Nemir never really recovered. From then on, he focused purely on survival. He didn't want to take chances, he didn't want to grow. He wanted nothing exciting to happen to the firm. He'd been through enough.

A CRISIS OF CONFIDENCE

The financial implosion set off a cascade of crises for the firm. In addition to the massive losses in its capital, Investcorp faced write-downs (which reduce the value of an asset but assume the asset still has *some* value), write-offs (which negate all present and future value of an asset), and downgrades by ratings agencies.

For the first time in its history, Investcorp was forced to systematically cut staff. All the departments were asked to provide a list of names. About fifty employees were laid off; in a firm of fewer than 400 people, everyone knew someone who was leaving. That something like this could happen in a small, entrepreneurial firm accustomed to success was shocking and demoralizing.

As well as shaking the firm's financial foundations, the traumatic experience crippled people's confidence. "No one in our generation"—investors who came of age during the 1990s bubble—"had ever seen a crisis of such severity," Daniel noted. "There was a lack of confidence at all levels—among both individual professionals and the investment committees. We kept asking ourselves, 'How can we be sure this investment will provide a decent return? Do we really know what we're doing?'"

In addition, there were deep concerns about the health of the companies that Investcorp had acquired for its investment portfolio. Of the ten companies in the firm's European and U.S. private equity portfolio, six were not performing. "We were thinking, we're going to lose *all* the equity," Daniel recalled.

Certainly, some of Investcorp's clients were wondering the same thing. Herb Myers, who is now the co-head of Investcorp's real estate business in North America, recalled investors angrily yelling at him, "I gave you my money! What do you mean there's no equity left in the building at 280 Park? It's your headquarters!"

Many clients had lost faith in Investcorp. There would be no new real estate deals in 2009 and only a tiny number in 2010. Some 80 percent of Investcorp's Gulf-based real estate clients defected to other firms. "We had to develop a new investor base in the Gulf and rebuild our credibility," Herb said.

And then, just as the United States began to emerge from the financial crisis, in 2010, the Eurozone was hit by its own debt crisis.

Private equity firms make money by doing deals: they collect transaction fees when they buy a company and, assuming the company has increased in value, when they sell it. Investcorp's European private equity arm didn't do a single deal for *three* years—2009, 2010, and 2011. Daniel compared Investcorp's state of mind to a once-great soccer team that has been so beaten down it starts to doubt its own abilities: "When you haven't scored a goal in years, you start to wonder, *When you shoot, will the ball even go in the right direction?*"

"The company was treading water," Tim Mattar observed. "We weren't sinking, but we weren't moving forward. There was no real strategy, no real vision, no real business plan. Just 'more of the same.'"

Many people, even among the Investcorp faithful, couldn't help but begin to wonder. Maybe "more of the same" was no longer good enough?

THE FOUNDER'S CURSE

Anyone who knew Nemir Kirdar would say without hesitation that he was a brilliant man. His idea of creating a boutique investment firm providing a bridge between the Middle East and the West was visionary for its time. The deal-by-deal model of private equity investing was spot-on for the mentality of Investcorp's ultra-high-net-worth Gulf clients. And not only was it unique; it also worked, magnificently.

But times had changed.

In the 1980s, Investcorp was one of the first firms to venture into the new asset class of private equity, opening the door for other firms that would specialize in this area. These other firms—firms like Blackstone, the Carlyle Group, Apollo Global Management, and TPG—were all founded after Investcorp. But they took a different path; they committed to a fund model. That enabled them to grow bigger and faster than Investcorp.

As I described earlier, one fundamental way in which the fund model differs from the deal-by-deal model is that investors—either individual investors or, more often, institutions—commit a certain amount of capital to the fund manager to be invested over a certain period of time, usually five years. The significant element is that the investors do not know any of the companies the manager might buy. That's why these investment vehicles are called "blind pools."

There's another, even more significant difference between the two models: the fund model is very scalable; the deal-by-deal model is not.

Scalability is the magic password that enables growth and profitability to a massive degree. You're probably familiar with Archimedes's famous quote, "Give me a place to stand, and with a lever I will move the whole world." That, in a nutshell, is the concept of scalability.

In the financial industry, the real-life version of Archimedes's lever is a fund.

Here's how it works. Every firm starts from the same place: Fund I. It has no track record as of yet, so it is the toughest to raise committed capital for and, consequently, is the smallest. After five years, though, assuming the fund has done well, the firm will have credibility and can leverage that credibility into subsequent funds. Fund II will be bigger because the initial investors will come back for more and new investors will want to join them. Fund III will be even bigger and Fund IV bigger still. Now, these funds are so enormous that it makes sense to spin off additional funds that invest in specific market segments. So, now these fund "families" are sprouting more and more branches on their family trees, with each new branch benefiting from the success of its predecessors and attracting greater and greater amounts of committed capital. In 2022, for example, Blackstone launched its tenth global real estate fund, BREP X, initially targeted at a capitalization of $25 billion.[6] And that's just one fund, in one specific market.

An even more significant factor: The source of the capital for these funds is the worldwide institutional base of banks, pension funds, labor unions, and insurance companies, rather than individual investors. In other words, it's limitless.

Investcorp's deal-by-deal business model, by contrast, was not scalable. To be sure, there's no shortage of wealthy individual investors, but you source your capital in smaller chunks because you're dealing with private clients, not institutions.

Even before the financial crisis, Nemir refused to consider anything other than the deal-by-deal model. "Nemir believed that it was our differentiator, what made us unique. His thought was, 'If we go the fund way, we'll be one of many. I'd rather be the only one,'" Tim explained.

Perhaps if Investcorp had faced stiffer competition on the deal-by-deal model, Nemir might have been more open to starting the fund model much earlier. (Investcorp now offers a variety of funds and is aggressively courting institutional investors, as I discuss in chapter 8.) But it was the unquestionable leader in the Gulf, which only confirmed Nemir's bias toward the deal-by-deal model. "He didn't want to hear about the fund model," said Tim. "It became taboo."

It was a classic case of "the founder's curse," said Yusef Al Yusef, who joined Investcorp in 2005 and is now head of Investcorp's private wealth platform in the Gulf. "We'd talk to Nemir about what regional competitors were doing, what the multinational financial firms were doing. They were doing much bigger transactions and raising far larger amounts of capital. He wouldn't listen. He wanted to continue the model. We were stuck in the past. But what about the future?"

"In business, you're either growing or dying," noted Dave Tayeh, who is head of Private Equity North America. "Markets grow and your competitors grow." In comparison to Blackstone, whose fee-earning 2010 AUM was $109.5 billion,[7] Investcorp's AUM continued to hover just under $10 billion.[8]

In the wake of the financial crisis, Nemir doubled down on the deal-by-deal model. He had filled the hole in the balance sheet by convincing investors to provide a $500 million infusion in preferred equity, but the firm was paying 12 percent interest for that lifeline—every year. The only way to slip out of that shackle was to grow enough to pay back the amount within five years. But there was no vision for growth; it was only of returning to and maintaining the way things had been before the cataclysm. Meanwhile, the firm's profits were going to service the interest obligations on the preferred equity. The debt was eating up the firm.

Dave is an outspoken guy who doesn't mince words: "Investcorp wasn't just stagnating. It was dying." (Dave felt so strongly about the situation that he left the firm in 2011. He returned in 2015 to help us rebuild.)

"FOR THE FIRST TIME, WE WERE FACING SERIOUS COMPETITION ON OUR HOME TURF"

As a member of the Board of Directors, I had a front-row seat for Investcorp's struggles. And I was no mere spectator. I was actively involved in helping Nemir raise the capital that helped save the firm. (Abdul-Rahman Al-Ateeqi, the Chairman of the Board of Directors, was also instrumental in this effort. Almost all the other board members were a full generation older than I was and had retired from running their businesses. The investment world had evolved—state-owned sovereign wealth funds had become major players—and their contacts were no longer current.)

Investcorp tried to leverage its longstanding relationships, but with the global economy on the ropes, the whole world was looking for help from one of the few places that still had extra money to invest: the Gulf. For the first time, we were facing serious competition on our home turf. That gave Nemir even more concern—and made me realize that the pond Investcorp swam in contained lots of fish, many of which were much larger and far fiercer.

The firm clawed its way out of the maelstrom caused by the 2008 financial implosion and the Eurozone debt crisis with a deal here and a transaction there. The challenge was as much about rebuilding client confidence as anything else. When you sustain such a large number of losses, clients worry as much about the fundamental health of the firm as they do about the state of their own portfolio. And they doubt your ability to make smart investment decisions going forward.

Their uncertainty showed in the first private equity deal Investcorp did after the cataclysm, in 2010: a $70 million acquisition of Veritext, a New Jersey–based national provider of legal transcripts to law firms, Fortune 500 corporations, and regulatory agencies in the United States.

Veritext was exactly the kind of company we liked to add to our portfolio: it had such potential. And, in fact, by the time we sold it six years later, Veritext had doubled its sales force, completed sixteen strategic add-on acquisitions of its own, opened offices in two new markets, and become the premier brand in deposition services.

Yet when the Investcorp team initially tried to interest investors, for the first time they couldn't place a deal. Tim remembered a tense meeting when Nemir went around the table, asking each team member why they couldn't place the deal. "It's a difficult environment," people said. "Clients don't trust us anymore."

Nemir exploded. "Listen, you just gave me a hundred reasons why you couldn't place. You're here for one reason: to place. So place it."

"We got there in the end, but it was tough," Tim recalled. In happier days, placing this kind of deal would have been accomplished in just a few weeks. This time, it took a year. It was clear that the firm was not working at its full potential.

I could see that there were other firms, like Blackstone, Carlyle, Apollo, and TPG, all of which were created after Investcorp, that were using the Investcorp model to leapfrog beyond us. (I had read a lot about Blackstone when I was at Harvard, so Blackstone immediately came to mind.) More troubling was that when I met with people in the investment business, they'd say, "Oh, we used to look at Investcorp in the 1990s, but we don't now."

When the big people think that you're not relevant—and you're not even on their radar—that's very telling.

A NEW CHALLENGE

This was the situation when, in 2014, Nemir Kirdar asked me whether I'd be interested in succeeding him as Executive Chairman.

Obviously, I needed to think about it. I had left an intense job as the chief of the Royal Air Force of Oman a little over a decade earlier; sometimes it seemed like just months. I was still reveling in the freedom of having time to spend with my family and do the things I wanted. (Among other things, I had cofounded and had run Rimal Investment Projects, which connected high-net-worth investors to growth opportunities in Oman.)

But Investcorp had such great possibilities.

Nemir was always a bit chauvinistic about Investcorp's roots in the Gulf. He was proud that an Arab firm had become so successful. When he talked about Investcorp's future, he often said, "I want someone to take it forward but not forget where we came from."

That spoke to my heart. The Middle East is so often full of bad news, but here was something good that could be made even better. Restoring Investcorp was a good cause, a worthy task. That really appealed to me.

Investcorp was the only Gulf-based nongovernmental company that was as prestigious and respected as other Gulf-based global brands like Emirates Airlines and Saudi Aramco, both of which were government owned or affiliated. Much as being the chief of the Air Force had amplified my voice in military circles, taking on the Executive Chairmanship of Investcorp offered an influential platform in the world of finance. I was only fifty-three, too young to rest on my laurels. I liked the potential of this new incarnation to make a difference in my life and in the lives of others.

Lastly, my eight years on Investcorp's board had helped me see the enormous opportunities for the firm. In fact, during that time, I was often puzzled about why more people didn't see those opportunities and act on them.

Was it a risk? Absolutely. But taking risks is something I'm familiar with. I can't think of any riskier career than being a fighter pilot. In fact, my experience as a fighter pilot helped me assess the opportunity at Investcorp. If you want to survive as a fighter pilot, you quickly learn not to take risks without understanding the situation you're going into: the hazards and threats, how to avoid them, and if they're unavoidable, how to deal with them. The decision to become Investcorp's Executive

Chairman required applying situational awareness in a different arena, but the decision-making process was no different from the one I had applied in the Air Force.

Other people may have thought that Investcorp was in danger of becoming irrelevant, that it was on the path to being a has-been. I thought we could turn it around. And when you see an opportunity where you can make an impact and do good things, it's compelling—almost irresistible.

I was eager to take up the challenge.

CHAPTER 3

"WHY NOT $25 BILLION?"

I was not, perhaps, the obvious choice to succeed Nemir Kirdar. Although I had cofounded and served as the Chairman of Rimal Investment Projects, I had never been an investment professional. I had never run a hedge fund or a private equity team. My knowledge of alternative asset class investments came from serving on the board of Investcorp.

But Nemir wasn't looking for an insider. As he wrote in his memoir, he specifically wanted someone he considered a statesman, someone like David Rockefeller. "Such a person must be able to meet, on Investcorp's behalf, with the rulers of the Gulf countries. To do that, he must be accepted in the Gulf community as a very senior man. At the same time, because Investcorp's culture spans the Middle East and the West, he must also be well-received in New York and London."[1]

Nemir continued that he was searching for someone with an international perspective, an ability to navigate cultural, economic, and political waters anywhere in the world, someone with judgment, imagination, and foresight—"in other words, *vision*."

Nemir himself was a man of vision. You could see that in how he had constructed Investcorp's Board of Directors. Nemir had deliberately selected the original board members according to two criteria: they had to represent the entire Gulf region, and they must each be among the most trusted and respected leaders in their own business community. In a region where favoring family and friends is embedded in the culture, they had to be untouchable, their integrity unquestioned. Their reputations gave the young firm the blue-chip credibility Nemir sought.

Some of those old warhorses were still serving when Nemir invited me to join Investcorp's board. I was as unlike them as you can imagine. Many were in their seventies; I was a full generation younger. They came from business and banking backgrounds; I came from the military. They had helped build the firm; I was a complete outsider.

But I was eager to learn.

In retrospect, I think Nemir tagged me as a likely candidate to succeed him almost as soon as we met. Nemir was a great admirer of the British and U.S. Air Forces. They were known for instilling boldness, teamwork, and tremendous individual responsibility in their members. At the same time, they demanded painstaking attention to detail, extending from the thorough pre-flight checklists to exacting post-mission debriefing sessions during which the entire squadron discussed mistakes and how to learn from them. My Air Force background would have set his antenna humming from the get-go. Then there was the fact that I had a degree from the Kennedy School; Nemir revered Harvard. And I was from the Gulf.

Furthermore, thanks to my time spent at the Kennedy School, the Royal Air Force U.K. Staff College, the U.S. National War College, and the National Defense University, as well as the Royal Air Force of Oman, I had a large network of contacts among the military and governments in the United States and the U.K., as well as, of course, in the Middle East. I was honored to serve as an occasional emissary for Sultan Qaboos—a sort of unofficial ambassador. As icing on the cake, both Nemir and I were Brookings Institute Fellows and were both affiliated with the Eisenhower Institute. Those experiences checked off Nemir's "statesman" box.

When I first joined Investcorp's Board of Directors, Nemir went out of his way to make me feel comfortable on the board and in the firm. In the aftermath of the financial crisis, we spent a lot of time together: in

Bahrain, in London, at his house in the South of France. He invited me to big parties, like his birthday bash, and intimate get-togethers with heads of state and global business leaders. He used me as his sounding board to analyze the firm's strengths and weaknesses, as well as his concerns about its future. I guess he liked what he heard because he'd often say, "I don't have the relationship I have with you with anyone else on the board."

Although he never declared he wanted to retire, from the moment I met him I sensed he was seriously considering it. Obviously, the financial crisis deferred that decision. As the firm's founder and leader, he didn't want to abandon a sinking ship; he wanted to do the right thing.

But I remember a conversation we had over lunch late in 2009. By then, we had raised the capital necessary to save the firm, and things were slowly getting sorted out. He said, "I don't understand why you don't want to be more closely associated with the firm."

"I do," I replied. "But I don't want to do anything without your mandate. It wouldn't look good for you or for me or the whole firm."

From that point on, he encouraged me to join as many board committees as I wished and to visit Investcorp's offices around the Gulf, as well as in London and New York. Most board members didn't do that. Nemir wanted me to get to know the various executives and learn the firm's footprint in the industry.

I took him at his word—and then some. Years later, someone showed me a cartoon from a 1933 edition of *The New Yorker* magazine, showing two coal miners peering into a dark tunnel where a light in the distance is shining. One of them exclaims to the other, "For gosh sakes, here comes Mrs. Roosevelt!"—a reference to First Lady Eleanor Roosevelt's relentless determination to see first-hand how Americans lived and worked in every corner of the country. It sounded familiar. Firas El Amine, our global head of corporate communications, told me that he recalled two colleagues in our New York office reporting, "There's this board member who questioned us about tech funds for two hours." No board member had ever done that before. Upon hearing that the board member was me, Firas wasn't surprised, since he and I had already had a deep discussion about enhancing Investcorp's media coverage.

I also received guidance from two of Nemir's most trusted confidants: Betty Pires, the Chief of Staff, and Stephanie Bess, the General Counsel. Nemir could analyze the big picture, but these two women knew the details—the politics, the processes, the people. They had seen it all. Once they decided to take me in hand, it was like someone lighting a torch and leading me through a dark forest while pointing out all the pitfalls along the way that I might not have noticed.

For example, when Nemir talked about my succeeding him, his idea was that I could come in once or twice a month and schedule regular offsite meetings with the co-CEOs the rest of the time. He implied— quite strongly—that the firm could run itself. I thought, "This is a great arrangement!"

Stephanie set me straight. As a Black woman who had graduated *cum laude* from Harvard Law School, she was among the smartest of the smart. Direct and outspoken, she didn't hesitate to let me know how things *really* stood. I remember her saying, "Let me tell you, this is *not* going to be a drop-in-once-a-month job. There is *so* much to do. If you want to move this firm ahead, you need to make major changes in its operating structure, its profitability, and the Board of Directors. This is going to be a hard, hard, *hard* job."

Betty, meanwhile, was educating me on the nitty-gritty. Almost from the beginning of my term on the board, she suspected I needed to learn more and just *know* more. Betty had been with the firm from its very first "office" in a one-bedroom suite at the Holiday Inn in Bahrain, and Nemir trusted her implicitly. When she asked him if I should see a particular letter or get a copy of a brief, it was practically a formality. He always said yes. Betty didn't just send me papers; increasingly, she would say, "You must look at the terms of reference"—the implicit and explicit purpose and structures of a project, committee, or negotiation. "Don't just glance at them. Look at them seriously. Make sure they are right, because they'll give you the right emphasis to do what the firm needs."

Betty and Stephanie saw their roles as safeguarding Investcorp and shepherding its transition to new leadership. I knew Betty wouldn't stay—her career was closely tied to Nemir's—and Stephanie was thinking about retiring; but they did so because of their loyalty to the firm and to Nemir.

When you take on any leadership role, especially when you know you'll be instilling change in the organization, you want to have the humility to learn and to let people know you are willing to learn. When you show you're genuinely interested in learning more about what people do, they are much more likely to open up. You'll be inundated with information.

Some of the most valuable nuggets may not be factual, per se. To be sure, you want to know how people do their work. But you also want to tune your antenna to pick up the intangible elements: Do they seem committed to their jobs and the firm? What makes each person excited about coming to work? What prevents them from doing the kind of job they'd like to do? What—or who—are the stumbling blocks? What would they like to see done differently?

The other thing that's so necessary when you come into a position like this is having connections. You have to know the people you'll be dealing with, whether from past networking or from the fact-finding conversations you've been having. They will be your sounding boards and your safety nets, as well as the means to launch your vision. Your strengths and weaknesses will be magnified by *their* strengths and weaknesses. You want to use everyone around you to the best of their ability, for the best of the firm.

In my case, though, I had to do it unofficially. Even though I had Nemir's permission and blessing to investigate and ask questions, I had yet to be designated as his successor. I was still "just" a member of the Board of Directors, albeit an abnormally curious one.

It was an awkward position to be in.

"NOT THE USUAL TRANSITION"

Despite Nemir's firm intention to retire, he didn't know how to go about making the transition. He was like an artist who couldn't hand over his masterpiece. As long as he kept tinkering, he wouldn't have to acknowledge that his work was done.

So, even though Nemir and I had verbally agreed in 2014 that I would succeed him, there was no official announcement—not even an unofficial one. While I knew Nemir planned to float the idea with certain key shareholders, some board members, and the senior executive team, I didn't know when he would set things in motion. Nor could I even assume he definitely would. Every fighter pilot knows that the best-laid plans can shift in a millisecond.

It was not the usual transition, but there wasn't much I could do. It was Nemir's firm, and he was firmly in charge. While I was eager to get moving, I couldn't push him. The best thing was to just stay calm until he was ready.

Meanwhile, although I couldn't shadow Nemir as his designated successor, I could further my understanding of Investcorp by deliberately deepening what I had already been doing: familiarizing myself with the firm in even more detail, asking about and analyzing opportunities, and exploring how I, with my existing contacts, could enhance those opportunities.

Nemir finally announced his decision in January 2015—but only within the firm, not externally. It wasn't an official mandate, but it was a start.

Over the next six months, I further immersed myself in all things Investcorp. Because Nemir had kept me a secret, now I had to quickly jump on the knowledge wagon. I knew the firm from the board's perspective, and from my occasional conversations with employees, but I didn't really know the structure and processes that made it tick, the in-depth details of the different lines of business, and what people wanted and expected from the next leader. Learning that was my first priority.

Most leaders coming into a company from the outside find themselves in a state of temporary incompetence, faced with having to do the most at a time when they know the least. I'm not embarrassed to ask questions to get to the facts or to learn what I need to know. By nature, I'm a person who adapts quickly, but this was a big change for me and I didn't automatically feel confident I could succeed. I needed to remove any self-doubt by really understanding the firm and by identifying the skills, as well as the carrots and sticks, I'd need to do the job well.

To sharpen my situational awareness, I consulted a wide range of Investcorp employees and affiliates. In addition to talking to Nemir, the leadership team, and some board members, I made the rounds of Investcorp's different offices, buttonholing employees at all levels, picking their brains and canvassing their opinions. I wanted to speak with people who had been with the firm from the beginning, to get their perspective on the past and how we got to the present. And I wanted to speak with relative newcomers who could provide an outside point of view, compare Investcorp with the firm they had left, and explain whether Investcorp had fulfilled their expectations.

I continue to have these conversations today.

When I talk to our people, my inquiries fall into two categories. The first is professional: their career path and their thoughts about the business. How did they start their journey and how did they get here? What do they do, how do they do it, and where do they fit into the organization? Why is their business area important to the firm, and what are the key elements that shape success? Whom do they interact with, both horizontally and vertically? (That interaction with other lines of business is important: it tells you whether there's good communication and a supportive culture.) What is changing in their area of expertise? Is there anything we can do to make it better? What is working and what is not working? And, of course, how might we improve?

I also ask about the personal side: I like to know whether our people are happy to be affiliated with Investcorp. Will they encourage their friends to come work here? That shows they are proud of Investcorp and committed to it. And if they're not, I obviously want to know why.

These open-ended questions provide a lot of information and, equally important, give the people you're talking to the chance to discuss what *they* think is most important. When you get negative signals, of course, you have to verify what's behind them. We're human beings and we all carry baggage. So, you check and double-check to calibrate the reliability of the feedback. Gradually, a portrait of the organization emerges.

A recurring theme in almost all the conversations I was having in the first six months of 2015 was that the firm had stagnated. It was worded differently, but there was no doubt that many people thought the firm was treading water.

There was also a palpable sense of uncertainty. The financial crisis was tough on the firm. While there had been a decent recovery by 2015, it wasn't a V-shaped, sharp bounce back. People wanted to know, "Where is Investcorp going?" They kept hearing all these great stories about Tiffany and Gucci, but those deals were in the past. What was there to look forward to?

As I painted my canvas, I focused on the big picture, the strategic decisions: Why did we concentrate on acquiring mid-market companies in our investment portfolio? Where did we want to go with our real estate investments? What were the repercussions of limiting ourselves to investing in North America and Western Europe? Should we explore other markets and, if so, which ones? Had we maxed out our client base in the Gulf? Should we expand our client base and, if so, how? Should we expand our investment offerings and, if so, into what? How important was it to maintain our core identity as a firm rooted in the Gulf? How important was it to maintain our identity as a boutique investment firm? Could we expand without losing that sense of self?

$9 BILLION ISN'T BIG ENOUGH

Nemir didn't make his decision public until almost the last minute. From the date of the announcement, I had barely a month to prepare for my new role.

At that point, I could contact outsiders who had long-time relationships with the firm and their peers at other investment houses. With them, my questions were along the lines of: What do people in the finance industry think about Investcorp? Where do they position it in comparison to other investment firms? How much do we need to grow? Where are the opportunities for growth?

What I learned was that $9 billion in AUM was definitely not a size that would get attention on Wall Street trading floors and in plush Park Avenue headquarters. Investcorp called itself an alternative assets investment firm, but we didn't offer half of what was on the menu at other alternatives firms. We didn't have a line of business in credit, for example, or investment in infrastructure. We operated in limited geographies, with limited demographics.

The message was loud and clear: Scale was important, and scale comes from growth. The role models were right in front of us: Blackstone, Carlyle, KKR, Apollo. They had all been founded after Investcorp, and they all surpassed it in size. It was a strong verification that we needed to grow.

However, my vision for Investcorp wasn't just for growth: it was also about *how* the firm could turbocharge its growth. I believe that the fact that I came from outside the financial sector was an advantage. Instead of getting entangled in details, I could clearly see that Investcorp needed to unshackle itself from the constraints of being a boutique firm for investors from the Gulf. That idea had served Investcorp well for thirty-three years, but "boutique" automatically evokes upper limits in terms of size, scale, and scope.

Rather than discarding our past, we needed to use it as a springboard to launch the firm into new areas and attract new clients.

I believe that, in his heart, Nemir understood the necessity for growth, even if he couldn't wrap his head around it. His ultimate goal was to bequeath his creation to someone who could honor and preserve it, while lifting it to the next level. Even at that time, even though it wasn't too long ago, it was the rare Arab firm whose founder chose a successor who was not a son or a nephew. (Nemir didn't have a son.) He could have chosen anyone, but he chose *me*. I was honored. And I felt responsible for realizing his unspoken dream.

A MAP OF A NEW WORLD

I officially became Executive Chairman of Investcorp on July 1, 2015, a Wednesday. That same week, I sat down with co-CEOs Rishi Kapoor and Mohammed Al-Shroogi in the opulent wood-paneled conference room of our offices in Bahrain, its windows curtained against the blistering July heat. (Mohammed retired in 2018, then became a Senior Advisor; Rishi continues as co-CEO.) Thoughtful and deliberate, Rishi is probably one of the brainiest people in an exceptionally brainy company. It's a pleasure to watch him think.

I asked for their thoughts about our growth.

Rishi produced two sheets of paper. One mapped out a two-dimensional grid of markets that were relevant for Investcorp—North America, Europe, the Middle East, and Asia—and asset classes where the firm could make an impact: private equity, real estate, hedge funds, credit management, and infrastructure.

He had put Xs in the boxes to indicate where we were present and left blank those where we were absent. For example, the box for North American private equity had an X, but the whole of Asia was empty. Real estate had an X in North America, but nowhere else. The entire row for infrastructure was empty. Credit management was empty.

I was riveted by all that blank space. It represented so many opportunities! I felt like an explorer about to embark on a voyage to a new world.

The second sheet of paper was a rough sketch that Rishi detailed on the room's white board. It spotlighted adjacencies: leveraging an existing presence in specific geographies and asset classes to expand into other geographies and asset classes. For example, Rishi explained, "We have a thirty-three-year presence in private equity in Europe. Shouldn't we be doing real estate deals there, too?"

What emerged on the white board was a series of concentric circles. At the center of the circle was the core of Investcorp's existing businesses. The next circle outward represented new products, such as credit management and infrastructure, that Investcorp could offer in the geographies where it already had established a strong track record. The third ring outward indicated the completely new markets for Investcorp—namely, China and India.

That was the road map for growth, but what was the destination? And how would we finance the journey?

The markets and the firm had bounced back somewhat after 2010, but scars remained. Private equity was our best pipeline for raising capital, but the deal-by-deal model was holding us back: transactions came back slowly, and our ability to execute on those transactions was not what it once was.

The hedge fund industry as a whole had stabilized, but there was simply no appetite for hedge funds among our Gulf clients. What interest there was came from institutional investors, but even among them the focus had changed. Many institutions set up their own internal teams with more direct oversight; the whole concept of a pooled vehicle of different hedge fund managers—a "fund of funds"—shrank significantly. While we supported the hedge fund business with our own balance sheet, we struggled to make it profitable.

We were rebuilding our U.S. real estate business, but it was slow, hard work; we were almost literally rebuilding it brick by brick. We had laid the foundation, but people couldn't yet see how it would become a cathedral.

NEW STRATEGY, NEW BENCHMARK

Later that month, Rishi, Mohammed Al-Shroogi, and I sat down and made some rough calculations. If we approached the next leg of our journey with a view toward addressing the blank space on the road map, and developed a strategy to extend into adjacent businesses and geographies, first with new products in existing markets and then with existing products into new markets, where would that lead us in terms of the firm's assets under management?

"Nemir's focus was always on annual net income. He wanted to make sure we could generate that net income to pay our people and pay dividends to our shareholders," Tim Mattar recalled. "Other than in hedge funds, there was *zero* sense at that time of any AUM business."

Applying AUM as a benchmark of success was a significant shift, one that would be central to the new strategy. Previously, Investcorp had focused on transaction fees, which were generated when the firm bought or sold a company. While the business model had been successfully built around a regular flow of transactions, there was one flaw in the formula: Because the model is subject to economic and financial cycles, it is volatile and unpredictable. When transactions dry up, as they did in a big way following the 2008 financial crisis and the Eurozone debacle, the firm's revenues take a major hit.

Shifting to an AUM-based model had a variety of advantages. Most important, it translated into an emphasis on fees for assets under management rather than on transaction fees (although some income would continue to be based on transactions).

Management fees are predictable and significantly more stable.

They're the finance industry's equivalent of charging rent: you know how much money is coming in each month. That steady source of income enables you to create operating leverage, attract talent, scale your business, and, consequently, attract institutional investors—the ultimate goal among clients. All that combines to boost the firm's value, which in turn makes shareholders happy.

Additionally, the private equity industry—one of Investcorp's two foundational pillars, along with real estate—has always focused on AUM as *the* core benchmark: it's how firms measure and rank themselves against each other. It's an easily understood, readily tracked, and objective way to compare your progress and performance against other firms.

Size matters, as they say. The AUM figure reflects the size of funds that are launched and, consequently, the size of transactions you can execute within those funds. In private markets, the vast majority of products and strategies are built around committed capital. A fund life is typically twelve years: five years to invest the capital, five years to realize the investments, and an additional two years should some investments take longer to mature. That capital translates into AUM. The greater your AUM, the more predictable your revenue stream from management fees. The more predictable your revenue stream, the more attractive you are to institutional investors.

At the time, Investcorp counted some $9 billion in AUM, which I had learned was pretty small potatoes. We needed to boost our AUM. The question was: What was a realistic figure?

Rishi, Mohammed, and I noodled around with some figures. "Why not $25 billion? In the next five years?" I proposed.

$25 billion AUM in five years. It was an attention-getting number, more than double the firm's current AUM.

But as I saw it, it wasn't so much a moon shot as a natural progression. With private equity, every year you try to achieve 20 percent growth. That basically means doubling your value in five years—at least. My thinking, too, was that we should grow not just organically but also inorganically by acquiring new lines of business. When looked at that way, $25 billion AUM made sense.

It was an audacious goal, the kind of number that initially took your breath away. But we three agreed that it could be achieved. All that was necessary was a lot of hard work, a little bit of luck—and a complete reinvention of the firm's culture.

CHAPTER 4

"OH, MY GOSH . . . WE'RE MOVING!"

There's a saying that a leader without followers is just a guy taking a walk.

Just because you've created an itinerary doesn't mean people will join you on the journey. Transforming an organization's culture requires commitment from the top—and conviction from everyone else. How do you persuade people to shift from living in the past to thinking about the future? How do you instill an enthusiasm for change—and the fortitude to take the risks required to realize that change?

By giving people something to get excited about.

What I wanted our people to get excited about was not just the target of $25 billion. It was also what the target represented. What that figure represented was, to quote Barack Obama, "the audacity of hope." I wanted people to be inspired by the possibility of exceeding their own expectations. I wanted them to believe that, by working together, they could reach that goal. And I wanted them to trust me to lead them there.

I had presented the road map to Investcorp's Board of Directors in mid-July. They approved the proposed course of action, after which the two co-CEOs and I spent the next six weeks fine-tuning it. It would be announced at an offsite meeting of the Operating Committee—the OpCom—at the beginning of September 2015.

"GOOD ENOUGH" IS NOT GOOD ENOUGH

On September 1, fourteen people gathered at The Grove, the former estate of the Earl of Clarendon, which is now a luxury golf resort and conference facility just outside London. The strategy wasn't the only thing making its debut. So was the Operating Committee.

The idea for OpCom came from something I had started when I was leading the Air Force. Every day at 7:30 a.m., we would hold what I called "morning prayers" to go over the plans for the day. There might be up to fifty people in the room at the beginning of each session, both general staff and senior officers. We'd start with subjects of universal interest, then narrow the focus. As we zoomed in on a topic, the people who didn't need to be involved would be excused. We'd zoom in some more, and more people would leave. Eventually, it was just myself and three or four other people analyzing strategy and other sensitive issues.

By the end of "morning prayers," everyone knew what was expected to happen that day, what had happened the day before, what they needed to plan for tomorrow, what might go wrong, and how to sort it out if there was a crisis. It was a great method for bringing the whole group together.

I thought this setup was just what we needed to create at Investcorp. Obviously, you can't have "morning prayers" every day when your senior leaders and major decision-makers are spread across different geographies and time zones. My original idea was to schedule the meeting every two weeks, then move it to once a month.

That first Operating Committee comprised the executive team, the heads of our different lines of business (at the time, Private Equity North America, Private Equity Europe, Real Estate, Hedge Funds, and a Gulf Private Equity business) and a select group of other senior leaders, including the Chief Financial Officer, the Chief Administrative Officer, the General Counsel, and the Head of Risk Management. (The number of members would vary over the years as we added new lines of business and focus points shared by all lines of business, or LOBs, such as environmental, social, and governmental concerns.) The size was smaller than the Managing Directors Group and larger than the Executive Committee. That was intentional: I wanted to create a forum for discussion, where everyone's voice could be heard and their opinions noted. I made it clear when I sent out the agenda that the purpose of the OpCom meetings was to share information and exchange views. Thus, OpCom was not a decision-making body; that was the responsibility of the Executive Committee.

The members all knew each other, of course, but this was the first time they had been brought together to work as a unified team—if possible. When a company has been stagnating for so long, maintaining the status quo becomes its own mandate. There's a kind of institutional inertia that takes hold, a "good enough" mentality that creates a real barrier to change.

I suspected many people at Investcorp didn't see any need for major change. After all, by 2015, the firm had rebounded from the double-barreled hit of the 2008 global financial crisis and the 2009–2010 Eurozone debt debacle. In fiscal year (FY) 2012, the firm raised $214 million in capital for private equity and $132 million for real estate investments; in 2013, the figures were $494 million for private equity and $201 million for real estate; in 2014, there was another increase to $571 million and $285 million, respectively; and in 2015, private equity notched a whopping $788 million and real estate hit $307 million.

The firm was doing well enough at $9 billion AUM. People were happy enough. Stagnation wasn't necessarily unsatisfactory. One person described the mindset as, "I'm comfortable enough. Why should I change what I'm doing?"

My concern was the mentality that protecting the status quo had created. Stagnation spawns silos, and silos in turn reinforce stagnation—it's a vicious circle. We'd dug ourselves out of the hole, but we weren't going anywhere.

"Good enough" was *not* good enough.

STUCK IN SILOS

Silos can sneak into any organization. They start gradually. Companies need specialist departments and closely knit project teams to get their work done, to provide focus and accountability. But then the groups develop their own identity, with their own habits and idiosyncrasies. It's a natural human response, and it isn't all bad. In some cases, this cohesion helps encourage esprit de corps, boosting productivity and efficiency.

However, groups sometimes become protective of their resources, especially during tough times like those we had just emerged from. In a company like Investcorp, one of the most valuable resources is knowledge.

What happens when business groups cannot or will not share information, ideas, and personnel across administrative lines? When people are trapped in silos, they look inward, rather than outward. They don't know what their colleagues in other departments are doing. They can't benefit from the knowledge others have amassed. They don't have a sense of what the company as a whole stands for, let alone how their work aligns with the company's greater goals. They don't see the big picture.

What happens next? In the absence of knowledge, people start making assumptions about other groups, and even about the organization as a whole. It's all too easy to suspect co-workers in other departments of acting for nefarious reasons. After all, if you don't talk to them or see them or work with them on a regular basis, it's natural to assume the worst in their intentions.

Silos become breeding grounds for negativity. Politics fester, and people start working against each other. Instead of expanding their situational awareness, their focus narrows. Instead of seeing clearly, their vision is clouded by blind spots.

You can imagine the effect. Companies lose their ability to connect the dots. They no longer spot opportunities or, if they do, they refuse to share the resources to take advantage of them. They fail to anticipate threats, or if they do anticipate them, they lack the ability to communicate their concerns broadly and quickly. In a world in which change is the only constant, they're unable to respond rapidly.

I'm not saying that Investcorp had reached such a dire situation. But as an outsider, I was able to bring a new perspective and see the direction in which we were heading.

In 2015, Investcorp clients could choose among product offerings in three asset classes: private equity, which was divided between North America and Europe; real estate, which focused entirely on North America; and the scarred hedge fund business, which was also U.S.-based. Each business was defined by its geography, which was, unsurprisingly, territorial, each LOB fiercely defending its limited resources at the first sign of a threat. The business silos were further reinforced by their separate locations in New York, London, and Bahrain.

Investcorp was competitive, quite rightly so. It had never fostered the kind of "you eat only what you kill" culture typical of many other financial firms, but people had fallen into the habit of "everyone for themselves." I'd noticed that teams didn't know what the other teams were doing; an initiative from one line of business was unfamiliar to another LOB. Everyone had their own perspective, and they weren't always conscious of other perspectives.

There was certainly little or no sense of a broader platform or the potential for firm-wide synergies. That was another challenge the silos presented: how to get people to understand that they were part of a larger context, that the firm's success as a whole takes priority over individual achievements.

Ironically, one of Investcorp's core strengths—the mix of cultures that enabled its deep understanding of different markets—had become a major stumbling block. Nemir Kirdar had intentionally built a cross-cultural, cross-geographic leadership group, but there were intrinsic culture clashes that the silo mentality sharpened. For example, Gulf people aren't brought up to be confrontational, while Americans tend to be forthright in their opinions, so Americans sometimes accused the Europeans and

Gulf people of not being straightforward, while their European and Gulf counterparts felt the Americans were blunt and pushy.

The Operating Committee was going to be my instrument to bridge the divides and break down those silos.

SHARING THE WEALTH

Before our first meeting, I sent everyone a copy of Gillian Tett's book, *The Silo Effect*, about the dangers of building departmental fortresses and the benefits of breaking down barriers. The implicit message was: Yes, we need silos of expertise, but we must identify and put in place explicit strategies to communicate with each other and share information among those silos.

For that first OpCom meeting, the information I wanted everyone to share was about as basic—and as important—as could be. In the agenda I sent out, I asked everyone to submit to the group in advance a report on what was happening in their line of business: the status of the portfolio; what they were focusing on and why; the growth strategy; the challenges and opportunities; the resources required to meet the challenges and realize the opportunities; and how other branches of the firm could help out and benefit.

It sounds so simple, but it was so profound. Sharing the information and discussing it educated everyone about what their colleagues were doing, and it pushed them to consider how their own LOB fit into the larger context of Investcorp. By "everyone," I meant everyone: at the end of the day, all the non-investment services—legal, administration, finance—needed to know what was planned in the different businesses so they could best support them. It was the first step in encouraging everyone to start thinking like a team.

Each OpCom member presented an oral summary of their report, then we discussed what we had just heard. The OpCom members were a smart bunch of people, very confident. They all knew each other, some for decades. Having an open dialogue was one thing I definitely wasn't concerned about.

(Initially, the OpCom meetings always began with these reports— circulating the written reports before the meeting and the oral presentations during our time together. After about eighteen months of refining the format of the reports, to reduce unnecessary information to a minimum, I said, "Let's assume that everyone is reading what was sent out, so in our meetings let's focus on what's strategic." Today, because we have so many more investment teams, there are about 150 pages of presentation material in the OpCom decks. Obviously, everything can't be an equal priority.)

Teamwork was critical to the success of the whole strategy. It would either make or break what we decided on. That was my main goal: to ensure that everyone now sitting around the table at The Grove would continue to sit together in their mind and spirit afterward, to work as a team rather than as individuals. I didn't want them to pay lip service to the idea of collaboration, then go back to the office and forget about it. I wanted all the leaders aligned and working together; only by visibly acting as role models could this new mindset filter throughout their groups and change everyone's behavior.

To that end, the OpCom meetings were scheduled to be held in person twice a year, with video conferences every month in between. The frequency of the meetings was something new; previously, Managing Directors meetings had taken place only once a year.

Never underestimate the power of proximity. I was counting on the simple mechanism of forcing people to spend time together on a regular basis to help build a broad *and* cohesive team, one able *and* willing to overcome differences and work together. I didn't feel I needed to make speeches about this. Simply by ensuring that there was frequent opportunity to interact, to get to understand each other's points of view, OpCom could—and would—become a powerful tool for coordination, communication, and collaboration among members themselves and between them and the senior leadership and me.

In fact, that ended up being the case. The monthly frequency was a small but significant way to help the team come together and align individual interests to reach a common goal.

ACKNOWLEDGING THE ANXIETY

Transitions are always periods of anxiety, but in this case the concerns were especially high. For thirty-three years, Investcorp had been founder-led and founder-driven; no one sitting at the table had known a leader other than Nemir Kirdar. Nemir had a larger-than-life personality, with enough charisma to overwhelm a room, with some to spare. By contrast, I tend to be a listener and an observer. Few on the Operating Committee had spent much time with me before I officially became Executive Chairman.

Then, there was the fact that I had a different background. I knew people were asking themselves, "How will his military background translate into the alternative asset management business?"

For most, I was a completely unknown quantity.

In addition to a change in leaders, there was also a new leadership structure to adapt to; instead of one person indisputably in charge, there was now an Executive Chairman and two co-CEOs. The dual-CEO structure had been introduced by Nemir in April 2015. Investcorp had a history of co-leaders: co-heads of hedge funds, co-chief operating officers, and the like. Nemir liked that balance. I also suspect that he thought two CEOs from inside the organization would make a good counterweight to an Executive Chairman hired from outside. And it's a well-known axiom that a three-legged stool is inherently more stable than a two-legged one.

But the new structure raised questions: What would be the roles of the two co-CEOs? How would the power be shared? As "the new broom," would I start cleaning house? Would there be layoffs or, at the least, a restructuring?

Then, too, there was the inescapable knowledge that the firm had been stuck in low-growth mode for far too long. The recent influx of capital had helped the firm recover lost ground, but little else had changed. The fundamental way the firm operated was still the same. Would that continue?

I opened the meeting by acknowledging the uncertainty. "I know this is a transitional time," I said. I emphasized that I was not coming in to revolutionize the firm. Rather than fire people, I would focus on building shareholder value. And, I made a point of stressing that I was willing to learn.

"You came off as calm, even-handed, and ready to listen," recalled Jonathan Dracos, the then head of the real estate group. "You promptly tackled the new leadership structure. I remember you firmly saying, 'There can be three people with the top titles but only one with the vision. It will be a collaborative vision, but my job is to set the overarching vision and the job of the co-CEOs is to attend to the details.'"

It was time to share that vision.

"IF YOU DON'T GROW, YOU DIE"

The vision, I announced, was growth: not incremental growth, not slow and steady growth, but extraordinary, exhilarating, and to some, I knew, what seemed like unrealistic growth. It was my job to convince them that it could be done and that *they* could do it.

When launching a transformation, it's critical to give a shock to the system. It's a way of indicating that the change starts *now*. People were comfortable following the same, familiar path. It was time to jolt them out of their comfort zone.

"Why do we have to grow?" I asked. "The answer is simple: in this industry, if you don't grow, you die."

The need for growth wasn't a question of bigger bragging rights or boosting our egos, I explained. It was purely existential. For thirty-three years, the firm had done the same thing, and while we had done well, other firms that followed our lead had done better—much better. We couldn't expect to continue doing the same thing for another thirty-three years and succeed—or even survive. I repeated, "If you don't grow, you die. If *we're* not growing, we're dying."

I think that simple punchline flipped the switch. No one wants to be part of a dying organization.

"Let's not spend the next three days going through all the details of the business updates," I said. (People tended to submit PowerPoint decks the size of a small novel.) "We can read the update decks later. We should only be discussing strategy—how to double or triple each line of business."

That was something new and, to many, completely unexpected. "Nemir's belief was that we should remain a boutique firm, tapping a select group of investors mostly from the Gulf," said Hazem Ben-Gacem, then the head of European private equity. (He became co-CEO with Rishi when Mohammed Al-Shroogi retired in 2018.) "This was the first time we had this kind of approach."

There were more surprises to come.

Change is scary; that's a given. Managing change is a skill, one that has to be built up and worked at. You wouldn't expect a swimmer accomplished at clicking off laps in a pool to do well in an open-water competition: the strokes may be the same, but the strategy of swimming in a scrum, of sighting in the absence of lane lines, the mental strength required to respond to changing wind and water conditions—all these demand a complete shift in training. You have to develop the muscles and mental capability to adjust.

At Investcorp, once the firm had righted itself after the shocks of the financial crisis, there had been no real challenge to the status quo, so the intellectual and emotional capabilities to accept and even welcome change as an opportunity for innovation were slack.

In a way, that's not surprising in this business. This is not an industry that's comfortable with doing something new. Investing is all about risk management; calculating risk is at the core of our success. We take high-stakes positions, and people can make a lot of money—or lose it—accordingly. The idea of "successful failure" that's so crucial in the technology industry just doesn't fly here. Thomas Edison's quote that "I have not failed. I've just found 10,000 ways that won't work" may be an acceptable thing to say in science, but it is absolutely the wrong thing to say to a roomful of potential investors.

In the past, anything that deviated from Investcorp's tried-and-true model was routinely squelched. Should Investcorp expand its client list into Asia, or should it target government-investment entities in countries like Kazakhstan or Azerbaijan, which were awash in oil money as the Gulf had been in the 1970s and, like the Gulf, were not yet being served by European and American investment firms? The idea would be dismissed with the comment, "Our client base is in the Gulf." Or, someone might propose launching the kind of blind pool funds that were a hallmark of Blackstone, Carlyle, KKR, and their ilk, only to be reminded that Investcorp was known for its deal-by-deal model.

I understood that before the global financial crisis, there was no need to experiment. After 2008, the firm felt too vulnerable to stray from the beaten path, even if that path had become a well-worn rut trapping us.

Now those guardrails for safe operation were gone. I was asking for the development of a new mindset and new muscles. That would require laying down a foundation of trust—not just in me but also in each other.

When you're challenging the status quo, trust is absolutely paramount: It both greases the gears and is the glue that holds everything together. You cannot effect transformation without trust. Transformation requires speed, and speed depends on trust. It's only when you achieve this alignment that you can execute your vision.

I hadn't yet shared the $25 billion goal, let alone the fact that I was thinking even bigger, but I had introduced the vision of growth. Its strength was its simplicity. Let's do more of what we're doing: expand into adjacent platforms and geographies; raise more money from the Gulf; raise money from institutional investors; study how we can launch in India and China, because clients had been asking about it. Everyone could understand that.

Everyone could also understand that even though I proposed the vision, it was not about me but, rather, about what the firm could do. Investcorp doesn't anoint stars, so there were no personal gains or individual gains to be had. We would all benefit, but we would *only* benefit if we broke down the silos and worked together. That realization also helped build trust.

When you take on a leadership role—any leadership role—people will follow you if they believe you will help them fulfill their ambitions, whether those ambitions have to do with learning new skills, expanding their influence, or as is often the case in this industry, making more money. That's why it's so important to articulate the vision, to say, "This is what we want to achieve." Because then people can coalesce around achieving that vision. After all, there's no one who doesn't want to better their life.

LEADING FROM BEHIND

Whenever possible, I prefer to lead from behind. That may surprise some people, who assume that military leaders are always out in front of the troops. When you think about it, though, you don't expect an army general to be in the trenches or an air force commander to be in the air with a squadron. They're most likely to be found in the ops room, evaluating the whole situation and making decisions.

Leading from the front is appropriate when circumstances require a role model to take charge and personally set the tone. (I describe such situations in chapter 6 and, especially, in our response to the COVID-19 pandemic in chapter 10.) But when trying to effect change, especially the first time, you cannot charge off, racing down the track, and assume that everyone will keep up with you; that's a surefire way to lose 90 percent of your people. Nor can you force them to go down the same path; that breeds resentment, especially among entrepreneurial people, which in turn gives way to recalcitrance and even outright antagonism.

When you want people to take ownership of a new idea, you have to *give* them ownership. It's up to the leader to set the vision and describe the strategy, but then the leader has to step back and let people adopt it and get on with it. That way, they innovate on their own; they don't wait for the leader to think for them.

(I like to read military history. It's interesting to learn that Napoleon's early successes were based on the fact that he gave his commanders the authority and flexibility to react to the situation. He started losing only when he became more directive.)

Of course, you don't want people to flail about, trying to figure out the right direction. That's counterproductive and does nothing to reinforce your leadership. Indirect leadership is all about influence, about making your ideas and intentions known but giving people the chance to get accustomed to them and assimilate them—and the choice to do so. You point out the path you think is best, but you let them decide to take it.

Leading from behind has been compared to a shepherd pushing his flock forward: the sheep go at their own pace and they have a tendency to wander. So, there's going to be a lot of discussion and debate, and it's up to you to gently steer the conversation back on course. And it definitely helps to have a couple of sheepdogs—that is, trusted aides—to keep the discussions moving forward, on the path you want. (That was another role I envisioned for OpCom.)

I should say right now that this sort of indirect leadership is anything but efficient. It's time-consuming and it demands patience and complete attention. For example, when you're chairing a meeting, instead of jumping in with what you believe is right, you actively listen. You encourage people to share their opinions and discuss them. They may raise points you hadn't thought of. But when the discussion is finished, *then* you say what you want to say and point out the direction you want to go.

This is why leading from the back works best under nonthreatening, nonurgent conditions.

You have to judge whether a situation is best suited for indirect leadership. For example, if there's not enough impetus, people can get bored and lose momentum. You have to ensure that there's plenty of communication and connectivity on all sides to keep everyone moving ahead. That's the disadvantage.

There are disadvantages to leading from the front, too. If you're too far forward of your flock, a gap can develop between what you're seeing and thinking and what your team is doing. You don't give people a chance to think and create *with* you. They're always playing catch-up.

So, it's a delicate balance. But when the circumstances are right for leading from the back, the rewards are priceless and the skills learned are essential. As our global footprint expands, we want our people everywhere to have the confidence to innovate on their own. We need them to think for themselves, even if they make mistakes, rather than to get into the habit of waiting for their manager to think for them.

I saw our meeting at The Grove as OpCom's first exercise in collaboration and cooperation. Building those muscles, getting comfortable emerging from their silos and working together, they would learn to trust each other and the senior leaders—that was more important to me than efficiency.

For us, our path forward was indicated by the road map and the idea of exploring adjacencies. I presented the concept, then opened the discussion by saying, "I'm going to ask everyone a few questions. I want to understand the art of the possible."

I invited each person at the table to be bold: "How do we grow our business? How can *you* grow *your* business? Where do we want to be? What are your current statuses and main challenges? What resources would you need to grow the way you want?" I explained that I wanted all the departments to have real clarity on each other's performance and how they could help each other achieve our goals.

It was no secret that I didn't come from a finance background. I let everyone know I would ask a lot of questions: I was counting on them to educate me. And I wanted them to educate each other. I encouraged them to ask questions of each other and to share the best practices they had honed over the years. That knowledge transfer would benefit everyone: the more information that's available to everyone, the less likely anyone will operate in a silo.

THE ART OF THE POSSIBLE

That kicked off three intense, exhilarating days of brainstorming: What would we like to do and what *could* we actually execute?

Trust weaves a web that becomes both a safety net and a trampoline. At that meeting, everyone was finding their voice—it took a couple of years for OpCom to truly coalesce as a group—but even so, what they achieved that first day was truly remarkable.

Tim Mattar, who at the time oversaw capital raising in the Gulf—in other words, he was responsible for persuading our Gulf clients to fund our investments—later observed, "What struck me was that we had a group of people sitting around a table for the first time, and you saw all sorts of ideas coming out of them that you had no idea had been there."

Tim had joined Investcorp in 1995, so he had worked with everyone in the room, some for two decades. Now, he said, "You got to see a new and different side of your colleagues. We'd each been so focused on a very narrow pathway that that was all we expected from each other. The fact that they had all these other thoughts was fascinating. You realized that your colleagues had more depth than you had thought."

The conversations didn't center on "this deal" or "that deal." They took on a much broader perspective: the economic environment, the industry context, investment trends in private equity and real estate, what we should be doing in these areas, and which areas and industries we might want to look into. "These were different conversations from the ones we'd been having before," Tim said.

One recurring theme of the discussions was this: How can we do more? How can we do bigger deals? How can we do greater volumes?

If we find more deals, can we find more clients willing to invest more money?

We dug into the details for each line of business—the advantages and disadvantages. There were many. For example, European real estate was a natural extension of our U.S. real estate portfolio, but what should we focus on—development, repositioning, or Core Plus (the industry term for good-quality properties that needed small operational tweaks, such as making minor improvements, managing expenses, pushing up occupancy from, say, 90 percent to 95 percent, to fully optimize revenue). In the United States, our knowledge was in the Core Plus area, which produced steady, more predictable but not spectacular returns. Could we execute the same strategy in Europe and the U.K., or would our clients prefer a higher return on their investment, which typically comes from refurbishment, repositioning, and development? And who should lead this new line of business?

If we wanted to develop properties, did we want to concentrate on greenfield—that is, building brand-new facilities from the ground up—or on brownfield, which involves repositioning an existing building? Greenfield development carries different risks, because you tie up returns until the facility is built and rented out. Brownfield has another set of choices and potential returns, depending on how much value you add—whether it's modernizing the bathrooms, kitchens, and communal areas in old residential buildings or doing a gut renovation that transforms a commercial space into luxury condominiums.

That was just part of the discussion about European real estate. We had similar conversations about building a presence in Asia; expanding our fund offerings in the Gulf (back in early 2008, before the financial crisis, we had raised $1 billion for a closed-end fund to invest in Saudi Arabia and the rest of the Gulf); acquiring a private bank in Europe to access European capital; moving into the collateral loan obligation (CLO) credit business; launching regional and sector-specific funds in addition to the technology fund we already had; and scores of other ideas.

As we went through the possibilities for geographies and lines of business, we put together a list that got longer and longer and longer. By the end of the first day, we had a list of between seventy and eighty different things that we could do. It was a promising beginning.

SETTING PRIORITIES

The next morning, we examined the list through the hard lens of reality. There was no way we could do all these things: it's not humanly possible and, anyway, we were a small organization and needed to concentrate our energy and expertise.

All small organizations confront this question when they want to grow. It's a matter of how to allocate your resources. In our case, our resources were people and time. Deciding which to prioritize was a chicken-or-egg conundrum. You need profitability to hire more people to deliver greater returns, but it takes time to produce the profitability required to afford the new hires. You can solve the conundrum if you have unlimited capital, but we didn't have unlimited capital.

If the first day was all about theory, the second day was about setting priorities and practicalities: What did we think we could actually execute? How would we actually do this stuff? Who would be responsible for which goal?

That second day, we screened the ideas and decided what we should focus on and what we should put aside, either to look at further down the road or to dump in the dustbin. Our first consideration was identifying areas where we had expertise that could transfer to another geography. Another element was determining what areas—either geographies or businesses—we *had* to be in. (Credit management immediately came to mind, which I describe in the next chapter.)

We also spotlighted investments that had seemed like a good idea at the time, but in retrospect made us scratch our heads and ask ourselves, "How did this fit into what we're doing?" Take retail. Investcorp had done astonishingly well with Gucci and, to a lesser extent, with Tiffany's and similar luxury brands. So, when Sur La Table and Paper Source came along (in 2011 and 2013, respectively), the thought was this: It's retail and distribution, and we like retail and distribution.

Sur La Table was (and is) a U.S.-based specialist distributor of high-end kitchen equipment. In addition to selling well-known brands like Le Creuset and Cuisinart, it had its own line of products. Furthermore, select stores around the country offered cooking classes, which seemed like a great mechanism for bringing people into the shops and motivating them to buy things. Paper Source, too, while selling merchandise from other companies, had its own line of products customized for every occasion, from birth to death and every holiday you could think of.

By 2011, it was clear that the internet had revolutionized retail. Because of their strong proprietary brands, both Sur La Table and Paper Source seemed well suited to prosper online. And these were both businesses that appealed to Investcorp clients. Because, at the end of the day, the deal-by-deal model has to satisfy two components: you need to make sure from an investment point of view that the transaction is absolutely the right thing to do, and you need to ensure that you can raise the capital.

No one seemed to realize that shoppers prefer to put their hands on kitchenware or to physically feel paper goods before buying them. Plus, establishing a strong online identity demanded much more capital than was originally calculated.

Dave Tayeh had returned to Investcorp in 2015 as the head of U.S. private equity. When he looked at these businesses, he wasn't optimistic. "We'll do the best we can," was all he could promise. Sur La Table and Paper Source both declared bankruptcy during the COVID pandemic.

On the other hand, the growth of online retail boosted our real estate portfolio, as we began moving into industrial warehouses. Warehouses are basically big sheds. They're neither high-cost nor high-maintenance properties. They exist to house machinery that manufactures something, like the industrial bakery described in chapter 6, or to collect goods that then get distributed to consumers. (Think Amazon fulfillment centers.) Given the trend in online shopping, they seemed like a good idea in 2015. They seemed an even better idea five years later, when the COVID pandemic almost sank bricks-and-mortar retail.

At the OpCom meeting, it became clear that we had to shift out of B2C—business-to-consumer, or retail—and into B2B, or business-to-business, meaning businesses that supply services and products to other businesses. More than that, we wanted to focus on so-called CapEx-light enterprises: companies that don't require a high level of investment (aka capital expenditure) to maintain existing capacity or promote future growth. That eliminated manufacturing, which requires expensive machines, and hotels, which cost a lot to set up and require a minimum level of occupancy to be profitable. That became a guiding principle for us and has served us well, as illustrated by Fortune Fish, described in chapter 10.

By the end of that day, we had a short list of priorities. From there, we had to address a key question for each promising item on the list: Do we buy it or do we build it?

Our business was buying companies—that's what our private equity teams did all the time, so we knew how to do it—making them better, and then, a few years later, selling them. There's a whole raft of challenges to consider if you plan to acquire a company for keeps: Is it a good cultural fit for you? How can you help it grow? You're buying human talent, so how do you ensure they get integrated properly so that they stay and prosper? (Our acquisition and integration strategy is discussed in more detail in chapter 6.) The stakes are even higher if you're acquiring a new line of business.

The genesis of our three existing LOBs was organic. Acquiring a new LOB requires an entirely new mindset; it requires thinking on a much larger scale.

Our sort of investing is often perceived as being the purview of bean counters and quantitative analysts. In fact, we are a people business, so we wanted to bring on board people whose vision matched our vision. Similarly, our cultures had to mesh; we had to share a similar philosophy.

There were other elements to consider, too. Because you're buying for your own balance sheet, that affects how you'll fund the acquisition: Do you do it with equity, with debt, or do you borrow extra to make the acquisition? And is there a decent enough spread on what you think the returns will be on your investment and the cost of funding it? What will that mean for your balance sheet if you're going to do more of this sort of thing? Because the Investcorp balance sheet had historically been used for underwriting its transactions, what portion were we willing to set aside to make additional acquisitions?

Building something ourselves raises its own set of issues. The biggest is that it takes a lot longer to put all the elements in place. Could we transfer expertise from one geography to another, or would we have to find a new leader and hire a new team? There's a steep learning curve in either case. While you're learning the ropes, the payoff from your first transaction will be relatively small.

Proposing ideas, debating the pros and cons, prioritizing the next steps—the whole process was a way to test the theory underlying our road map. Also, by inviting everyone to share their insights and reactions, I wanted the team to feel ownership of this journey of growth—that it was *their* personal mission and that they understood the only way forward was to work together.

Just as I hoped, the process began to coalesce OpCom into a collective body, with the capability to clear difficult hurdles in a collaborative manner.

"WE HAVE OUR TARGET"

By the third day of our meeting, I felt we had made good progress.

Now, I asked everyone: "Are your responsibilities clear?" I wanted all the departments to have complete clarity on each other's role and how to support each other to deliver on the strategy. The only way the road map could succeed was if everyone concurred on how to proceed along the path, allocating resources, setting timelines, and identifying present and future pressure points. Only then did I say, "Okay, we have our target. It's $25 billion in AUM in the next five years."

I sensed some doubt, but not outright recalcitrance. But I could also sense a simmering excitement. I had thrown down the gauntlet. People were eager to pick up the challenge.

Not everyone was in favor of using AUM as a yardstick, though. A lot of people argued, "That's not a profitability number. Shouldn't we focus on profitability?"

AUM, however, is a target everyone could understand. It anchors a wide group of people and interests in achieving a clear, tangible goal. And there's real value in posting the numbers and constantly moving them up. You could critique it, but it's an effective tool.

My tone may have been matter-of-fact, but everyone knew that achieving that goal would require *massive* change. We'd have to move from a boutique firm with three locations to a truly global, diversified, alternative investment platform that wasn't afraid of growth. Jon Dracos recalled thinking, "I'll have to change my thinking and my group's thinking. We'll have to think outside the box about growth."

Tim Mattar had a more elemental reaction: "Oh, my gosh . . . we're moving!"

"IT'S *NOT* TRADITIONAL"

Two months after the meeting at The Grove, on November 4, 2015, I unveiled the vision at the annual investors' conference in Bahrain. In the audience were Investcorp's core clients: representatives from high-net-worth families and family offices; wealthy business people; members of Gulf royalty. Some had bankrolled Investcorp at its inception. They knew Nemir Kirdar and endorsed his boutique investment approach.

The meeting was as much my introduction to this key constituency as it was a public announcement of the new path Investcorp would be taking. It was a high-stakes moment. Once the vision was made public, there would be no going back.

"Over the medium term, we aim to more than double our current level of assets under management," I said. "We will build out our market positions across our business lines around the world. We will strive to innovate our product set to create diversified portfolios across multiple markets."

There was silence as the clients took it in. Then the room erupted in applause. When I sat down, one of the guests at my table leaned over and said to me, "This is a good plan because it's *not* traditional."

We were on our way.

CHAPTER 5

CHANGING THE MINDSET

I f you visit any Investcorp location today, you're likely to spot the same framed poster in someone's office, whether you're in London, New York, Mumbai, or Bahrain. The poster is a photographic collage of the intricately decorated doors of Oman.

Omani culture prizes its entryways. The doors of a house reflect its owner's personality. They can be artfully carved out of wood or sculpted in hand-hammered copper, painted in a kaleidoscope of bright colors, inset with stained-glass panels, or adorned with wrought-iron curlicues. The combinations of materials, colors, and decorations are endless.

The posters were a gift from me. They express my pride in my home country, but they also send a message. I wanted to remind people that our business is about opening doors to new opportunities. There are so many options available to us, if only we have the ability to see them and the courage to take them. By sending the posters, I was asking our people, Which doors will you choose to open and which will you decide to walk through?

A PLAYBOOK FOR TRANSFORMATION

I have always believed that people react to a fundamental change in one of three ways: they embrace it and come with you; they're not sure but are open to being persuaded; or they can't deal with it and have to be let go. My team and I focused on the large and ambivalent group in the middle. OpCom—both the meeting and the members—was a microcosm of Investcorp. It provided a preview of what to expect when we presented the vision for transformation to the rest of the company.

There were people who were eager for change, people like Dave Tayeh. Dave had left Investcorp in 2011; in early 2015, he came to Oman to discuss the possibility of returning. He asked me, "What do you want to do with Investcorp?"

I said, "I want us to grow." He was so happy. He said, "I left this firm because nothing was happening." Dave is now the head of Private Equity North America.

Very few people said to my face, "I don't think this will work." But I could tell there were people who were saying, either to themselves or among others, "This guy is dreaming. It took us thirty years to get to $10 billion in AUM. Now he's talking about $25 billion in five years? What is he thinking?"

Others were ambivalent. They didn't try to dissuade me, but they wanted to know how strongly I felt about our new direction and how many others might back me. *Then* they would jump on the train—and maybe even help propel it forward.

So, how could we deal with the inevitable pushback and inertia? How could we inspire people throughout the firm to sprint, not run, and to go the extra mile? How could we convince them that they were smarter, stronger, and more capable than they thought? What follows is the playbook we used to reshape the mindset of the firm, moving it from defending the status quo to exploring the art of the possible.

Shock the system. The goal of $25 billion AUM was announced to the entire firm at my first town hall meeting, held one month after the first OpCom meeting, in October 2015. As I did at The Grove, I wanted to wake people up—to shock them into realizing that we were marching along a path to irrelevance if we didn't change and start to change *now*.

The message was this: Investcorp would no longer be a boutique firm doing what it had always done. The focus would be on growth. Things would be different. They would *have* to be different. It was a question of survival. I repeated what I had said at The Grove: "If we don't grow, we die. That's a simple fact in this industry. So starting today, we will be pushing forward. We want to be at $25 billion AUM in five years."

I think the OpCom members, because they ran the various lines of business, were more aware of the fact that Investcorp had been treading water while other firms were blowing past us. However, I suspect that many of the other employees had no idea of the danger we faced. And why should they? With the exception of the year spent recovering from the 2008 global financial crisis, Investcorp had been solid and prosperous for all of its thirty-plus years. It *looked* solid and prosperous, with its wood-paneled offices and Persian rugs.

My announcement shook the foundations of their world. It was scary and disruptive.

I was just getting to know the OpCom members. I was a complete stranger to most of Investcorp's employees. I would have to rely on the business leaders to amplify the message and introduce our growth strategy; more than that, I would have to trust that their teams trusted *them* and would follow their path.

Jon Dracos, who then headed our real estate arm, later described his approach: "Basically, I said to them, 'We need to change the way we're thinking. What we're doing is nice, but it's a niche business. If we're doing transactions of less than $1 billion per annum, we'll now need to deploy $5 billion per annum. And we'll need to diversify our geographic footprint and our investor base, because we're too concentrated in the Gulf.'"

Real estate had always operated with a lean team, made even leaner by the layoffs after 2008. It had started to find new investors and re-establish its credibility, but as Herb Myers, the co-head of Real Estate for North America, observed, "between 2011 and 2014, we were taking baby steps."

Now the team was being asked to take giant leaps. The prospect, Herb recalled, was stressful, even overwhelming. "I was the head of acquisitions at that time, so a lot of that growth would be my team's responsibility. It was clear that we would be stretched thin."

"There was a lot of resistance at first," Jon said. "I spent a lot of time reinforcing to people that the growth strategy would have tremendous rewards for both the firm and the individual. Good investment professionals are highly motivated by rewards and by working for a growing, dynamic group. So, there was a lot of emphasis on compensation as well as on the personal journey of transformation: 'You've been *here* but you can get *there*. We'll help you accomplish that.' That's what eventually pushed people to change their mindset and buy in."

Question the status quo. Supporting the status quo is dangerous. You think, *We're doing fine because we're doing what we've always done.* Meanwhile, the world around you is changing, but you don't notice because you're comfortable following a familiar formula. Even worse, when you become set in your ways, complacency creeps in; you think you know it all and lack the energy or ability to push the envelope. Instead of being ahead of the pack—or even in the middle—in reality you're going backward because everyone else is passing you.

If you want to grow, you have to be willing to try new things. You have to welcome new ways of thinking and new people who bring new perspectives. Only by asking different questions can you see and open different doors.

I'd opened one such door before at the Royal Air Force of Oman, when I brought women into the Air Force. From the beginning of his reign, Sultan Qaboos had pushed for women to become educated and to take on larger responsibilities. They had responded wholeheartedly. In just one generation, a tidal wave of talented women poured into professional roles, becoming doctors and engineers and teachers, and taking positions in government, where they could shape policy and inspire the next generation of boys and girls.

I wanted to tap that talent pool for the Air Force. It wasn't easy, of course. Like all raw recruits, the women needed a lot of training—even more so because the cultural barrier had to be broken. Like all pioneers, they needed special support and role models. Fortunately, we brought on an Irish woman who was a military officer and had worked for the Jordanian Royal Flight. She shared her knowledge of what women needed to succeed as cadets, both with the leaders and with the women themselves. Knowing that we wanted these women to succeed gave them the confidence to push themselves—to volunteer to take different training courses and sign up for different jobs. (I left the Air Force before women became fighter pilots, but those initial classes of women did produce transport pilots.)

Bringing women into the Air Force was important in building confidence across the country, too. Throughout Oman, anyone— male or female—now knew there was no ceiling for their talent. The sky was literally the limit.

At Investcorp, setting the goal of $25 billion AUM similarly broke the status quo. A goal that big sent a big message. Stating that the goal was possible gave people confidence they could achieve it. Yes, it was a shock initially, but ultimately it energized them to break habits that were holding us back: habits like nostalgia.

You see, Investcorp had a bad case of nostalgia that was propping up the status quo. Nostalgia is an insidious drug because it pulls you into the past. The firm's successes with Tiffany and Gucci were landmark deals, and they were worth talking about. But they had occurred twenty years earlier. You can be proud of your history, but you can't keep living in the past. We had to break that nostalgia habit and focus on the future.

To do that, we needed to start thinking in terms of scale.

Scaling up is not a concept everyone is comfortable with. To use a military analogy, some people prefer guerrilla warfare; others prefer gorilla warfare. The former relies on surprise and agility; size is a disadvantage. The latter leverages size to overwhelm the enemy; bigger is better.

We had been thinking like a boutique firm. Now we needed to think like the big guys.

Our initial concept of scaling up was simple: expand into the adjacent white spaces on the road map. That's a good thing, but the truly transformative power of scaling up manifests itself when you can increase the size of the transactions, when you can take your core platforms and make them bigger. We weren't ready to do that yet. We had to build our muscles to lift heavier weights and gain the skills and confidence to do so. But that was the ultimate goal.

There are many advantages that come from scale.

Scale gives you options. When you have scale and you're hit with a financial crisis—or with COVID—you have room to maneuver. If you're hit, you can take it. You can afford to make mistakes because you have a safety net that will catch you and enable you to bounce back.

Scale enables you to target your objective in different ways.

Let's say we want to enhance our relationship with some of the big sovereign wealth funds in the Gulf. In the past, we could bring them opportunities only in private equity. Now, we can bring them a fund that invests in infrastructure in the region. Or, we can raise a fund specializing in local private companies that we can take public. Without scale, we can't do that.

People mistakenly think that scaling up increases your costs because you have more offices with more people. In fact, if you leverage the synergies of scale, your costs go up, but your revenue goes up even more—and your AUM goes *way* up. Done in a focused way, scaling can actually be very profitable.

You can scale up in two ways: organically and inorganically. You can grow bigger on your own, or you can grow through acquisition. Some people think the two are mutually exclusive. They're not. We would do both.

I was able to leverage my perspective as an outsider to question the way things were done. That perspective enabled me to ask not just Why? but also Why not? For example, why not develop a fund model in addition to the deal-by-deal model? Why does it have to be an either/or situation? Why can't it be both? Why can't we try something now that didn't succeed before?

One of my most persistent "why" questions was this: Why is Blackstone bigger than we are? I tended to focus on Blackstone because I had studied the firm intensively at Harvard's Kennedy School and have followed it ever since. At the time, Hazem Ben-Gacem said that was like the CEO of Rolls-Royce asking why they weren't as big as Mercedes. But I explained, "I don't want to be compared to small firms in the region. Blackstone, Carlyle, and KKR *are* our peers, even though our AUM is smaller."

I wanted people to realize: "This is the level we want to be dealing with. So, this is the level we must prepare to deal with."

Investcorp's identity as a boutique investment firm had

intrinsically limited our options and our future. You can't scale up by doing lots of small things. You have to make big moves. As I said earlier, you have to open your mind to new possibilities—and help everyone else to do the same.

Push people to think bigger. Hazem likes to tell a story of how he got the wake-up call that things would be different. It was at one of our first get-acquainted meetings. "At the time, I ran our European private equity and technology businesses," he recalled. (He's now the co-CEO.) "I thought it would impress Mohammed that we had secured a $25 million commitment from a blue-chip Asian sovereign wealth fund to invest in our technology fund. I was over the moon that they had committed $25 million to us, and I expected Mohammed to feel the same way."

Instead, Hazem remembered, I paused, then asked, "Why not $250 million?"

I wasn't being critical. I was genuinely curious. But Hazem went on, "His question made me think, 'Why *not* $250 million? And what will we need to do to get there? There's no reason that we can't aim to match the biggest of the biggest, and we should aim to go down that path.'"

Hazem concluded, "I came to realize that's typical of Mohammed's leadership: setting the target—a benchmark of 10×—but leaving it to the team to make it happen. That's when I realized that the only constraints were the ones we set on ourselves."

Pete Rommeney, our head of human resources, calls that epiphany "career crack." "Once you get that feeling that you *can* think bigger," he said, "you're hooked."

That was exactly what I wanted. But I knew there were people who weren't comfortable with the idea. They're used to paddling around in their own little pond; swimming in the ocean is scary.

You need more than a cheerleader to instill a growth mindset.

You need tools that nudge people into a new way of thinking about Investcorp and about the part each person plays in helping us grow.

In addition to the OpCom leaders setting the tone and tweaking the firm's compensation policy, our communications strategy became much more strategic, both internally and externally, so that everyone—throughout the firm—would get the message.

To begin with, we strengthened our internal communications. Town halls were a new concept at Investcorp. People knew about them, of course, but the firm had never held one before I became Executive Chairman. People had to be educated about the purpose of the town halls and how they operated; they had to be encouraged to participate. (I'll discuss how we did this later in this chapter.)

Investcorp hadn't had much in the way of an intranet or held meetings across lines of business. By bringing together people who work in different parts of the firm—both different functions and different geographies—the town halls helped break down the silos.

Over the years, we've expanded that concept outside of formal town halls to informal get-togethers. For example, Dave Tayeh is based in New York. It used to be that when he came to our Bahrain headquarters, he would meet with the Executive Committee, chat with a few colleagues, then fly back to the United States. On a recent visit, however, we organized a meeting with about forty people for him to discuss a fund he is leading.

As Investcorp began participating in more external events, we noticed a dichotomy between how we were viewed by outsiders and the perception from the rank and file. We deliberately used communications to elevate our external profile internally by publicizing our activities and achievements in *The Review*. Conceived as a small internal newsletter, *The Review* comes out twice a year and emphasizes the broader community in which Investcorp operates. It features descriptions of our star portfolio companies, has interviews with CEOs of portfolio companies, offers introductions of new hires, profiles the members of our International Advisory Board, and runs articles about events and initiatives that the firm is involved with. That's another way to shift people's perspective of Investcorp from a boutique firm to an increasingly important player on the global stage.

In addition to these soft tools, we used hard tools to force people to reassess themselves. Annual performance evaluations were a good opportunity to shatter the status quo. For example, in addition to their performance objectives and business objectives, people are expected to describe areas for personal development. I remember some people left that section blank. I put a big question mark in the space and sent it back. The first guy called and asked, "Do you have something in mind?" I replied, "No, but when someone says they don't need any personal development, it raises questions."

I'd noticed that people were grading themselves as star performers when they had achieved only what they were supposed to achieve. In my book, if that's the case, you are not a star performer. You have met your objectives. If you have exceeded your goals, then you've accomplished more than your objectives. But only if you have doubled or tripled what you were supposed to do can you *maybe* call yourself a star performer. People weren't happy, but they knew we had embarked on a tough, performance-driven journey. The firm had set a goal of more than doubling its AUM in five years. To achieve that, we would all need to outperform.

For our part, we had to create an environment that encouraged them to take risks.

Don't penalize risk-taking. I've always said that Investcorp will not be a one-mistake firm. If you want people to think bigger and to set audacious goals, they need to feel comfortable making mistakes. Otherwise, they will wait for you to think for them. That's the worst outcome for everyone.

Paradoxically, considering that we're in the business of taking risks every day, creating a welcome climate for innovation is really challenging. Pete Rommeney and I have had some interesting conversations about this. "Everything we do is heavily assessed for risk," Pete explained. "That's at our core. People in the financial industry are world-class smart. They're not used to failing, and they don't like it. By their nature, they're wired not to push things when they're not confident they will be 100 percent successful."

Despite the detailed calculation that goes into making an investment decision, throughout Investcorp's journey, obviously some decisions didn't pay off. We paid the price. But what we don't want to do is to point fingers. It's not one person's fault; it's a collective responsibility. And we make sure to make those disappointments look like that.

Trust is the key element in pushing people to break the habits that are holding them—and us—back. You have to be able to trust that your manager and the organization have your back if you challenge the status quo. People need to feel they're being cared for, they're not alone under pressure, they can talk to anyone—including me. They have to trust that when they do raise their hand, they won't be criticized or ridiculed or made to feel stupid for not knowing something.

We need to set people up for success. It's the leader's responsibility to keep an eye on how people develop and to give them the flexibility and opportunity to move, both vertically and horizontally. Clarity in setting expectations is really important. So is communication: how they're progressing, what challenges they're facing, and what tools we can give them to help overcome those challenges.

Once people see that thinking bigger is built into the culture, they feel more confident about stepping off the usual path. We've seen this not only in the different investment ideas they propose but also in how willing people are to learn new skills. And we're happy to encourage that.

That's been one of the secrets of our growth journey: we didn't bring in many new people to specifically manage this or that project; we drew on the talent we already had in-house.

Rotating people into different positions takes a certain amount of delicacy. You don't want to toss them into the deep end without providing them with the necessary skills and support. You want to set them up for success, not failure. So, we're not going to say to a real estate specialist, "You're a good investor in this area, so try private equity." That's a totally different business and mindset. But when we acquired 3i Group's credit management business (as I describe in chapter 6), we tapped Daniel Lopez-Cruz, who headed our European private equity business, to lead the acquisition team because he has good negotiation skills and due-diligence abilities. When we expanded into India, we called on people in Bahrain who had opened our offices in Saudi Arabia or Abu Dhabi and had experience building a beachhead in a new geography.

That's another advantage of scaling up: with a bigger global footprint, your people see bigger opportunities around the world to grow and develop, and they do things they haven't done before. Scale enhances and accelerates talent.

That's a huge confidence booster for everyone. Just as we're not a one-mistake company, one person's success is everyone's success. There's a famous World War II poster of Rosie the Riveter flexing her bicep and proclaiming, "We can do it!" That's the spirit I wanted to embed in the company.

Yusef Al Yusef was one of the people who was energized by the new mindset. An Investcorp veteran who had joined the firm in 2005, he told me, "I feel I'm a totally different person than I was five years ago. I don't feel as restricted as I used to be."

When we delisted from the Bahrain Bourse in 2021 (which I describe in chapter 11), Yusef was asked to represent Investcorp on three live television interviews. "Imagine going live on TV to defend our position," he recalled. "You don't know what to expect. But the fact that Mohammed said he trusted me to do a good job shows that he's willing to take risks on people. If something goes wrong, it's not the end of the world, and we'll try to do better next time. That allows people to grow and develop."

Not incidentally, that approach also makes you into a massive talent magnet, helping you both attract and retain talent. Imagine someone in private equity noting in his bio that he worked on the post-acquisition integration of a $10 billion credit business. That's what Habib Abdur-Rahman did: he started his career at Investcorp in corporate development and now he's our ESG (Environmental, Social, Governance) lead. Similarly, Roberta Vezzoli joined Investcorp as part of the European PE team, then shifted to technology investments. That kind of career path makes people look twice.

Of course, the firm will experience disappointments. No matter how much research and due diligence you put in, not every deal will work out. But that can help build confidence, too.

One of the most high-profile of these dead deals—the industry term for proposed mergers and acquisitions that go through all the due diligence but collapse at the eleventh hour—was our failed acquisition of the AC Milan football club in 2022, which became a matter of public record. The Rossoneri, nicknamed for the team's red-and-black striped shirts, are one of the most successful clubs in European football history, having won the European Cup seven times. Only Spain's Real Madrid had hoisted the trophy hardware more often.

We were willing to offer over $1 billion for the franchise. It would have been one of the biggest transactions in Investcorp's history. Admittedly, we were new to sports. Yusef, who as head of our private wealth platform leads our capital-raising efforts in the Gulf, joked that initially he didn't know a forward from a fullback. But we know about business, and our due diligence showed that AC Milan was a potential gold mine.

They don't just have customers; they have fans. The difference is that a fan is a customer who will stay with you from birth to death—and even beyond. Rossoneri season tickets are prized legacies to be passed from generation to generation. To put the power of the fan base in perspective, the New York Yankees are the most popular Major League Baseball team on Facebook, with over 8.5 million Facebook followers as of August 2022.[1] AC Milan has more than *500 million* fans worldwide.[2] They even have a fan league in Indonesia.

As things turned out, we were unable to reach a commercial agreement in line with our valuation assessment discipline, with AC Milan ultimately being sold to another buyer. Our dreams of football glory fizzled. But AC Milan opened our eyes to the opportunities in the sports industry. Who knows what future possibilities may play out that we would have dismissed before?

We celebrated that dead deal for the lessons we learned. Our challenge is to take the excitement involved when evaluating an unusual potential investment and spread it throughout Investcorp. To do that, you need to create an environment where people are honored for coming up with a groundbreaking idea. Too often, we recognize the innovative idea that worked, but we never hear about the other ten ideas that didn't pan out. Failing with good intentions has to be publicly celebrated; that's how people learn to be less risk-averse.

However, there's a very important caveat here: when someone messes up, it's absolutely crucial to understand the reasons behind their failure. Was it something within their control or did external factors influence the outcome? Should the firm have stepped in or was it more of a personal performance issue?

I tend to give people the benefit of the doubt. I think everyone is trying to bring value. So, when someone really fails, I want to know about it. Did they try something in good faith and get it wrong or is this a person who makes mistakes because they're careless?

When I was in the Air Force, there was a young trainee who was learning to fire rockets at a target while flying. Normally, you want to recover immediately after you press the Fire button. This guy wanted to see how the rockets had hit the target. He didn't realize he was hurtling at 1,000 kilometers per hour at a 60-degree angle right into the ground. (Talk about bad situational awareness!) He managed to pull out, and was promptly sent to me. I listened to his story. He explained that he wanted to ensure he hit the target before he flew off. He knew he was doing something *really* dangerous—and stupid—but he thought he had a good reason. It wasn't a good excuse, but he was a good pilot with lots of potential and this was his first mistake. He certainly learned his lesson and, because he acknowledged his bad judgment and promised not to make such a boneheaded decision ever again, I gave him a second chance. This was not a one-mistake organization!

Another time, though, I had a fighter pilot who decided to buzz a friend who he knew was going to be driving on a road near the base. Fortunately, he had warned his friend in advance, and *really* fortunately, his friend had parked the car and gotten out to take a picture as the fighter jet blew past. The pilot misjudged the distance and hit the roof of the car with one of the rear stabilizers. He was lucky that the plane didn't roll or crash;

instead, he managed to pull up and land safely. That stunt was careless, arrogant, and dangerous. It demonstrated all the wrong values. He was fired as soon as he landed, and he was out of the Air Force permanently.

Of course, we're going to make mistakes. That's how we learn, as individuals and as an institution. It's how Investcorp ended up being in the businesses we're in today—we learned from what didn't work. We just try not to make the same mistake twice.

Create a comfortable forum to share ideas. Respect for hierarchy is embedded in Middle Eastern culture, and under Nemir Kirdar's leadership, Investcorp was a firm with a deeply entrenched sense of formality. (That extended to the dress code. Men were expected to adopt the style of high-end Wall Street investment bankers: suit, tie, and Nemir's favorite Gucci horsebit loafers.) I wanted to ensure that people would be comfortable, both in what they wore and in how they communicated. I didn't want to be cloistered in the C-suite, hearing ideas or concerns only after they had been filtered and sanitized by layers of hierarchy.

The first step was pragmatic, although in the hierarchical Middle Eastern culture it was seen as revolutionary. At the end of that first town hall meeting, I put up the final slide. On it was my name—Mohammed—and my email address. I said, "Every one of you should feel free to send me an email if you think of something that we should be aware of." (Seven years later, people still talk about that and the fact that I encouraged them to break protocol and call me by my first name.)

I continue to maintain an open-door policy. I open the communications channel by scheduling one-on-one meetings with every new hire. I normally ask incoming senior-level people to give me their first impressions in a month—or two months, maximum—after joining us, before they're immersed in our systems and culture. When we bring quality people on board, we want to learn from their experience, so we want to catch them while the contrast is still sharp in their mind. I and maybe one of the co-CEOs or the person who previously held that role listen to their feedback and together we discuss what we can improve.

Whenever I visit Investcorp's offices, I go over the new-hire list with the local Human Resources heads, and we schedule fifteen- or thirty-minute meetings, depending on the level. I'll say, "I'm interested in what you think about the firm. After you've been here six weeks, send me an email on how things are going for you and what we could be doing differently."

At our town halls, I encourage people to approach me with a question, a concern, or even a challenge, if they want to. If they don't feel comfortable doing it in public, they can use my email. I think I've made it clear: I welcome *all* ideas.

I try to ensure that this mindset permeates the firm. One of our OpCom members had a bad habit of shutting people down when they came to him with an idea he didn't like. I said, "Look, the worst thing you can do is to say it's a stupid idea, even if it *is* a stupid idea. Because if you do, there will be *no* ideas coming to you from this person. If you don't like the idea, the best thing to do is just listen and say, 'Thank you.'"

That episode got me thinking about threats hiding in a different kind of blind spot. With the firm growing so quickly and working across so many different cultures, we need to sharpen our situational awareness in interpersonal relationships, to be more sensitive to the strengths and weaknesses of our colleagues. That's why I've encouraged more of our managers to take on personal coaches.

We're pretty good at eliminating blind spots in an investment environment. (I describe how we leverage our Board of Directors, International Advisory Board, and other members of our brain trust in chapter 7.) We want to improve how our managers and team leaders recognize their personal blind spots vis-à-vis other people. Coaching can be a useful tool to help brainy people enhance their emotional sensitivity and it makes them all-round better at their job. I think having time for people builds their confidence in trying new things. That's one of the best investments you can make.

Oh, yes, and if you look at the photos of the team on the Investcorp website, you'll see that many of the men choose to wear a dress shirt—without a tie. Some even wear a *thobe* or *dishdasha* in our Bahrain office. I do, too.

Make everyone an owner. One aspect of Investcorp's old-fashioned hierarchy that hampered culture change was the lack of shared ownership. In 2015, our employees owned less than 10 percent of the firm. I wanted to change that. My goal was for employees to own 40 percent of the firm.

Considering what we wanted to do, having nearly half the firm owned by employees would send a strong message to present and prospective talent that Investcorp was a true partnership—that everyone, even the most junior staff member, would be rewarded for the hard work they put into our growth journey and would share in our success. It also would send a message of stability to the marketplace: the firm's future did not rely on the wisdom—and whims—of one person. Considering some of the fundamental changes we had in mind, that endorsement would be key.

When you look at many of our peers in the industry, they are controlled by a small group that owns the majority of the firm. The idea of having 40 percent of a firm owned by its employees is truly unique. And, to give credit where it's due, that was Nemir's vision from the beginning—maybe not 40 percent, but he deliberately structured the financial foundations so that even he never owned more than 10 percent of the shares.

That was important, because no one person would have to relinquish their equity to divide it with everyone else. The shares came from the firm.

In 2015, those shares weren't yet available. They were still held by the firm's founders and certain outside investors. That would begin to change in the next few years, as certain transactions (which I describe in chapter 6) brought an influx of capital that enabled us to buy out those holdings.

Once we began to make shares available for distribution, our first offering, in August 2020, was over-subscribed. People wanted to buy more shares than the firm had to offer. Consequently, we had to limit that first offering to members of the Executive and Operating Committees; subsequent offerings were made in November 2020 to managing directors and principals; and finally, in September 2021, it was made to all full-time staff members, even the most junior drivers and receptionists. (We offered loans to the lowest-level employees to subsidize their purchase of shares.)

Today, I'm delighted to say that Investcorp employees constitute the firm's largest shareholder: We own close to 30 percent. As the firm began to grow, *everyone* could reap the rewards. That's a huge differentiator. When you talk to an executive assistant who is a shareholder, you can see the significance. That person isn't just holding down a job; they're an *owner*. Among the investment professionals, ownership shifts the focus to executing the growth strategy, rather than on accumulation of personal wealth. That tends to neutralize big egos or greediness.

Making employees into owners has changed their perspective. Now they have a reason to root for the firm, not just promote their career. Instead of working *for* the firm, our people *are* the firm.

All these elements promote engagement and empowerment. When people feel empowered, they're more likely to see the bigger picture and how they fit into it. It's the difference between merely laying bricks and building a skyscraper. When people see how their actions help deliver the firm's strategy, their mindset shifts. They think bigger. And the firm is gradually transformed.

Of course, the reinvention took time. As Jon Dracos said, "This was not a finger-snapping exercise." We had to work hard to overcome the inertia of our old ways and learn new habits. (We're still working on it.) But as the firm became more willing to stretch outside its comfort zone, one door after another opened.

People love to be where the action is. And we were taking action.

CHAPTER 6

THE FREE LUNCH IS NOW OVER

C oncept without concrete proof is merely cheerleading. A vision needs verification; otherwise it's as ephemeral as a mirage in the desert.

It was absolutely crucial to lay the foundation for Investcorp's growth platform and to do it as soon as possible, both to revive the firm's own confidence and to reinforce faith in Investcorp by existing and potential clients. That meant signing a few big deals—deals that not only were important enough to make headlines but also would be transformational for the firm.

"WHY NOT AIM FOR THE TOP?"

Even before officially becoming Executive Chairman, I had been quietly building a list of candidates who might be interested in taking an equity stake in Investcorp. At the top of the list was Mubadala Investment Company.

Headquartered in Abu Dhabi, Mubadala manages and invests Abu Dhabi's state funds, doing business on six continents with $284 billion in assets under management. (It's not a true sovereign wealth fund, like Norges Bank in Norway, KIA in Kuwait, KIC in South Korea, Temasek in Singapore, and others, but it essentially acts like one, so is often referred to as one.) Like Blackstone and Carlyle, Mubadala is one of the world's most respected financial institutions, the bluest of blue-chip names in the investment world.

Mubadala was involved in pushing projects that were reshaping the way the Gulf saw itself and how others viewed the region—renewable energy, Formula One racing, and tourism, for example. They were helping to establish a regional arts scene. Everyone knocked on their door.

I wanted to start our growth journey with a strong endorsement from the Gulf region. This was our home, after all, and how could we attract institutional investors from Europe or Asia if our own neighbors didn't recognize and back us?

"Why not try to get Mubadala on board?" I proposed. "Why not aim for the top? What do we have to lose?"

Investcorp had approached Mubadala before, but hadn't been able to come to an agreement with them, even during the glory years before 2008. In the wake of the financial crisis, most people inside the firm didn't even consider it a possibility. But Tim Mattar recalled that, around 2013, Nemir Kirdar remarked, "If anyone could convince Mubadala to commit, it would be Mohammed. He has the contacts, the position, and the credibility."

My appointment as Executive Chairman created a catalyst for change. In chapter 4, I said that whenever possible, I prefer to lead from behind. This, however, was a moment to lead from the front, to set an example by shocking the status quo and thinking bigger and bolder. I had told the firm and our investors that we wanted to reach $25 billion in AUM within five years. What better way to kick-start that effort than by bringing in new strategic investors? And, since I had set the goal, it was only appropriate that I lead the effort.

We reached out to Mubadala immediately after the OpCom meeting in September. They were interested, and by October 2015, Investcorp had started preparations for Mubadala's due diligence of us. This would be a deep dive that would determine whether they thought our growth vision was worth supporting. They decided it was, and at the end of July 2016, just a little over a year after I became Executive Chairman, the two firms jointly announced that Mubadala would acquire a 20 percent ownership stake in Investcorp.

The significance of Mubadala's taking that 20 percent stake in Investcorp was transformational, both inside and outside the firm. Within Investcorp, Mubadala's action anchored the new direction for the firm. It changed the minds of the naysayers who had claimed, "We won't get anywhere. We've tried it before, it's not going to happen." It made people realize that this was the level we wanted to be dealing at and it gave us the confidence to stretch to that level. The Mubadala transaction said, "This is a firm that is waking up and going places." It inspired our people to prove it.

One of the biggest impacts of the Mubadala transaction was that, for the first time in our history, Investcorp had put together a formal five-year plan. Mubadala had made it a requirement. They needed more than a promise that our vision would boost our revenues and bottom line, and therefore would increase the value of their stake. They required a real road map with actual details, not just indications of the direction we intended to go in. That, in turn, demanded a lot of deep thinking and detailed scenario planning.

Rishi Kapoor, our co-CEO, led the effort. He had previously served as Investcorp's Chief Financial Officer and had a fundamental understanding of the firm's potential. A business like ours relies on finding the right investment opportunities, but you need capital to make those moves. To continue the road-map analogy, if the firm is the vehicle, capital is the fuel that enables you to drive that vehicle into the future.

Rishi asked the different business leaders to provide their perspectives on possible growth, each backed up with different scenarios: "Jon, where can you grow the real estate business?" "Hazem, what are long-term promising trends in the Eurozone economy?" "Tim, do you think you can raise the capital for these placements?" He asked everyone to calculate the resources they'd need to expand, the cost of those resources, and how that would affect net income growth over the next five years.

In blending all the elements into a seamless strategy, Rishi had to balance top-down foresight: How does this get us to where we want to be?—with bottom-up planning: Can we actually do this? He had to take into account the fact that our investment environment was always changing, although that could be seen as an advantage. Asset managers like us can be nimble and move from areas where we perceive the growth potential has been tapped out to other areas with greater possibilities.

It was a lot like building a castle in the air, but the fantasy had to be grounded with a rock-solid foundation. This was 2016. The global financial crisis and the Eurozone debt crisis were well behind us. Still, we were walking a fine line between trying to be visionary and doing what we thought was executable. Ultimately, the plan had to be realistic. If we'd put fantastical numbers in there, it wouldn't have been credible. Mubadala had seen a lot of pie-in-the-sky plans; it was an expert at sniffing them out and shooting them down. Constructing the new road map was a massive undertaking, but it was worth every effort. It codified our goals and articulated our ambitions.

Another reason the Mubadala transaction was transformative was that Mubadala does not represent a high-net-worth individual or a family office. They are a true institutional investor. To be scrupulously honest, Mubadala was not the first institution to own a stake in Investcorp. Bahrain's Osool, which represents three different state pension funds, was the first, overseeing a 13 percent aggregated stake. But there is a significant difference in scale between Mubadala, a global institution, and Osool, which at the time was a single and much smaller pension fund. We hoped Mubadala's backing would persuade other institutional investors to follow their lead, and that was what happened. In the wake of the Mubadala transaction, a second Bahrain investment institution came into Investcorp's equity, with a 10 percent stake.

Mubadala's $200-plus-million stake gave us the resources to implement my vision. Prior to my becoming Executive Chairman, Investcorp was in large part owned by the first generation of founders, Nemir Kirdar and his original partners. Even after I became Executive Chairman, the firm was still essentially owned by the founding partners. They were getting older, though, and were ready to cash out. With the Mubadala money, now we could buy them out.

"That was the moment of transition of Investcorp's ownership from the first generation of founders to institutional ownership," Hazem Ben-Gacem later observed. "That's when the umbilical cord was cut."

Outside the firm, the Mubadala deal was a wake-up call for the entire industry. And the message was simple: You've been eating our lunch. But the free lunch is now over.

DOUBLING THE AUM OVERNIGHT

The Mubadala deal did more than represent the future for Investcorp. It also enabled us to begin to realize it.

The investment made possible Investcorp's second transformational transaction: acquiring 3i Group's debt-management business without breaking our balance sheet or compromising Investcorp's liquidity through debt financing or selling equity capital. Here's how it came about:

In 2016, we started looking at expanding into that second concentric ring of adjacent businesses: private debt management, also known as credit management. (It's the same thing, but credit management doesn't have the unpleasant connotation of thugs with baseball bats coming around to collect payment.) Private credit is a way for private—that is, non-public—companies to raise debt capital. Because they can't issue shares or loans to the general public, they turn to the private credit agencies, which lend money in exchange for interest payments and can impose covenants and/or collateralization terms that secure the loan.

The growth in private credit to mid-market and large-cap companies began to boom after the global financial crisis, as institutional investors looking for reliable income realized that there was an enormous universe of middle-market businesses actively seeking sources of non-bank funding. This asset class offered diversity across both geographies and industry sectors, and it had outperformed during the period of 2007 to 2010, which was the depth of the financial crisis.[1]

Furthermore, this was a universe that was expanding rapidly. Banks were consolidating in the wake of the financial crisis, and those that remained were much more cautious about how they used their balance sheets and to whom they lent money. Their belt-tightening left the private sector underserviced, forcing it to pay higher interest rates to gain access to capital. All this made private-sector lending even more attractive, especially to companies like 3i Group's debt management business, which had built global expertise in lending to private equity.

In short, private credit was—and continues to be—a massive market, and one we knew well. Investcorp put equity into our portfolio companies when we acquired them, but often our companies also took on debt to grow. We were familiar with how private credit worked because we used it ourselves—in fact, we frequently turned to 3i to supply it. Moving into private credit aligned seamlessly with our private equity growth strategy.

Lastly, what we particularly liked about the credit management business was that it was committed capital or, to put it in layman's terms, capital that you could count on. The underlying loans were typically issued for five-year periods, during which time they churned out a steady supply of interest payments, which were linked to interest rates and therefore floating.

There was another reason these loans were a reliable risk. When we talked about increasing our long-term committed capital, we looked for a business focused on collateralized loan obligations, or CLOs.

Here's a quick explanation: You've probably heard of collateralized debt obligations, or CDOs, which have a toxic reputation because of their role in the 2008 financial crisis. A CDO is a portfolio of thousands of loans—mortgages, car loans, credit card debt, and so on—that is financed by a stack of debt tranches, mainly in the form of rated bonds issued by the CDO and purchased by banks and other financial institutions. They rely on people being able to pay back their loans. When the housing bubble burst in 2007, and millions of over-extended homeowners defaulted on their rapidly rising adjustable-rate mortgage payments, the resulting crash in the value of CDOs and the overlying debt tranches was one of the triggers that caused the collapse of financial institutions around the globe.

Collateralized loan obligations, or CLOs, however, are primarily made up of hundreds of corporate loans, in the form of senior secured five-year floating-rate debt issues to private companies in a portfolio. The CLOs are financed by tranches of debt, but they are inherently less risky than CDOs.

The way CLOs work and the reason they're so attractive, Tim Mattar explained, "is that, unlike debt obligations, the loans made to private equity firms are a floating rate. If interest rates go up, the return on your loan goes up as well. That gives you a partial hedge against inflation. (Rising inflation rates boost interest rates, so you retain your spread, unlike bonds with fixed coupons, where the principal takes a hit.)

"Furthermore, these are minimum five-year loans that are the most senior of a company's obligations—that is, they are the first line to be paid back. The only thing you need to take into account is whether your borrower has the cash flow and assets to pay you back. So, it's all about their default rate and your track record of keeping defaults in your portfolio to a minimum. Assuming you've done your due diligence, and you can continue to display a strong track record of returns, you have what the industry calls 'locked up' or 'committed' capital, on which you earn management fees for the life of the CLO. It's another way to build up your AUM."

"We provide liquidity facilities," said Jeremy Ghose, who ran 3i's debt management business and now heads Investcorp Credit Management. Jeremy's connections with Investcorp go back twenty-five years. "Most of Investcorp's PE deals were leveraged buyouts, or LBOs," he said. "We provided the leverage in the LBO."

In short, the industry that lends to private equity firms was an industry we knew well. It had a close adjacency. As a globally diversifying investment manager, this was a space Investcorp needed to be in.

The next big question was, Should we build or buy our way in? You always have to take into account the cost of building versus the cost of buying. Can you afford to spend the time to hire the right team and nurture a growing stable of clients? Or, does it make more sense to buy a business with existing relationships with clients and investors? It depends on the sandbox you want to play in. When it came to credit, we wanted immediate scale. (When we launched in India, however, we did almost the exact reverse, as I describe in chapter 7.)

Rather than build a credit business from scratch, we decided to acquire an existing business. That was the very first time in Investcorp's history that we opened our mind to growing inorganically. That was another fundamental change.

Fortuitously, at the same time that Investcorp was starting to search for a credit management business, 3i was looking to divest its credit arm. Here's another important point: Investcorp and 3i tapped different pools of investors, who had looked to either us *or* them, depending on which investment strategy they needed to satisfy. Bringing 3i under our roof would enable us to switch that "or" to "and."

Lastly, Jeremy pointed out, "We were of size. We brought in 300 global investors and $12 billion in assets under management. That ticked the box."

It sure did. We announced the agreement to purchase 3i's debt management business on October 25, 2016. Overnight, we added a new line of business. Overnight, Investcorp's AUM more than doubled, to approximately $23 billion.

ONE CULTURE. ONE TEAM.

Jeremy and our people knew each other from years of doing business together. It helped that Jeremy and I shared—and still share—a lot of the same principles about culture and leadership.

"My first meeting with Mohammed was scheduled for one hour, but it was close to two hours by the time I left," Jeremy recalled. "I needed to be convinced that I was making the right decision—for my colleagues, our stakeholders, and the reputation of 3i. Mohammed was very calm, but he was passionate about onboarding us. He had a positive, clear vision, and he sold me effectively on the journey. He made me feel very comfortable that, although we would be the new kids on the block, we would be welcome, from the most junior to the most senior person. I remember vividly that by the time I left, I had made up my mind that Investcorp was the right home for us."

At Investcorp, though, we still had some misgivings—namely, we were concerned about the cultural strain of integrating an outside organization. Our people came from investment banks and had worked in private equity; once a client signs over the money, there is no further action until the investment is sold three to five years later. In contrast, the credit management business monitors books of loans—each CLO has well over 100 loans—any of which can be bought and sold in an institutional marketplace at any minute. The transaction aspect of private equity was essentially "Set it and forget it." Credit management was akin to day trading. Also, private equity, at least the way Investcorp practiced it at the time, was about personal relationships. The most significant partnership credit managers had was with their Bloomberg terminals.

Never in Investcorp's life had it accepted so many new people from a different profession, with a different business culture and different ways of thinking. Now, they would be part of the larger Investcorp family, and it was up to *us* to make *them* happy and comfortable doing what they needed to do.

Because it was in our interest to develop a successful and long-lasting relationship, everyone at Investcorp took a deep interest in ensuring that the integration was done as smoothly and considerately as possible. It was all hands on deck.

We had town hall meetings during which Rishi and Jeremy talked with small groups of teams—no more than twenty people at a time—to take their questions and answer their concerns. Our head of Human Resources sat down and met with every single person—about fifty people in New York and London—to introduce them to the firm. We established a buddy system to match the 3i people with colleagues at Investcorp.

"Culture is one of the biggest reasons that acquisitions fail," explained Habib Abdur-Rahman, now the head of Investcorp's sustainable investing strategy, but who at the time was tasked with leading the credit management's integration into Investcorp. "People tend to focus on where they will sit, how the technology works, what the security protocols are. That's important, and we communicated that clearly. But culture is usually left until the end. We focused on culture from the beginning. We wanted to get it right because we knew it would be relevant as we continued to grow inorganically."

What really messes with people during an acquisition is the possibility that their boss will change or their way of doing things will be changed—if they suddenly have to execute or report a different way. We assured Jeremy and his people that there would be none of that. They could continue to manage their business as they always had. The only thing that would change was that they would get our support to lift the team and grow the business bigger and bigger.

One thing we did immediately was to push the perspective that there wasn't a difference between the acquirer and the acquiree. That meant ensuring that every single person from 3i enjoyed the same benefits that Investcorp employees enjoyed. Their benefits had been lower than ours, so, yes, there was an additional cost, but the cost was worth it to realize our motto of "One Culture. One Team."

"It's always the little things that are memorable," Habib noted. "We made sure to do the little things, as well as the big things." On the first day of the new order, our senior team and I were there to welcome our new colleagues. We had a town hall at which we reiterated the reasons for the acquisition, explained their role in our new entity, and described how they would contribute to the growth of the firm. Participation from the top sends a message: When everyone sees the Executive Chairman personally involved, everyone is engaged.

Then our new colleagues were ushered into their new workplace. Their desks were organized, even down to the pens, pads, and staplers, with their computers and technology systems ready and waiting. Their Bloomberg terminals were set up and humming, so they could start trading from the minute they sat down. No one needed to hunt down tech support or search for a mislaid file.

"It's very difficult to integrate a group of fifty-odd people from London and New York, coming from different backgrounds and different cultures," Jeremy said. "But the whole process was seamless, from being greeted by the receptionist on the first day to being welcomed by the Executive Chairman with open arms. Mohammed made time to meet up with me in both regular formal updates and informal lunches and dinners. That was critical."

Whenever it made sense, we invited different members of Jeremy's group to accompany our teams on road tours to the Gulf to meet clients. And we benefited from their contacts, too. Jeremy is extremely well connected in Japan, from his time leading the group when it was part of Mizuho Financial Group. When we went on business trips together to Japan, there wasn't a single meeting where people didn't know him.

Slowly, slowly, "they" became "we."

What Investcorp brought to 3i's credit management was a focus on growing the business. We put pressure on them, of course, because we wanted them to perform. But we paid attention to them, to make sure they were looked after, well led, and rewarded, so that they *could* perform. The business has grown tremendously since. Today, the credit business accounts for over 40 percent of our $50 billion AUM.

"THE TIP OF THE SPEAR"

The 3i transaction sent the message: We're going to challenge the status quo. It demonstrated that Investcorp was willing to spend balance-sheet capital to build additional business platforms and push growth. It showed the art of the possible.

"That, in my mind, was the most transformational thing," Jon Dracos recalled. "We were no longer just a PE shop with a North American real estate business. So why not have another platform?"

One of the possible adjacencies that had been considered at the OpCom meeting at The Grove was an expansion of our North American real estate business into Europe. After the OpCom meeting, Jon had told his team, "We have a really good *little* business. We can have a really good *big* business. We can be the tip of the spear."

In the wake of the 3i acquisition, Jon had another message for his team: "We just bought a big business. So Real Estate has to get on board to be relevant inside Investcorp." Neil Hasson joined Investcorp in early 2016 to kick-start the European real estate business. "It seemed to be a natural extension of a very successful business model," he explained. "Mohammed had said, 'We've got a powerful franchise in Europe in private equity and a great franchise in the U.S. in real estate. Why don't we have a European real estate franchise?' That was the catalyst for hiring me and building the business."

Real estate is a very local business. European markets operate differently from the U.S. market. There are different players in each country, the lease structures are different, the buyer-seller interactions are different, and the regulations vary from country to country. Today there might be opportunities in Italy, but not in Germany; a year later, it might be different.

The very first deals we did were in the U.K. We decided to follow a specific strategy of investing in warehouses and logistics distribution centers. The U.K. had voted to leave the European Union in June 2016, and the referendum was reaffirmed by Prime Minister Theresa May in January 2017. Even though Brexit wouldn't go into effect for another three years, it was clear that the change would cause disruption in most supply chains, requiring more warehouses and distribution centers. We'd had experience in those areas in the United States, so we understood the sector well.

"We bought a big building in the north of England whose tenant was a large company that made cakes," Neil recalled. "When we analyzed the deal, the big risk was, If the cake business goes bust, can we find another tenant? (Fortunately, the British love their sweets, so that didn't seem likely.) A second building housed a business that made glass bottles. Glass is manufactured in a kiln, which you never turn off because it's too expensive to fire up again. So, the bottles were made 24/7 and were stored in another warehouse, which we also bought.

"The growth part was in how important the facilities were to the tenants. In both deals, what happened was that as the end of the lease approached, the tenants realized they were at risk. As the landlord, we had the leverage to adjust the rent to the market rate, which provided a more stable source of income."

The lesson we learned is that while you want to get the micro—the details—of a deal right, what really matters is the macro, or choosing the right sector to invest in. Then, the micro takes care of itself. For example, if we had bought shopping centers in 2015, no matter how much due diligence we did on the specific property, and no matter how good we might be at managing shopping centers, we would still have faced a massive headwind as the market subsequently shifted from shopping in person at bricks-and-mortar stores to shopping online. Looking back, it's easy to see that we would always lose that battle. But it wasn't clear at the time.

So much of successful investing comes down to timing and good luck. Fortunately, we chose the right sectors at the right time. Think of all those Amazon distribution warehouses that proliferated during COVID.

LONG-TERM SYNERGIES

Ideas sometimes emerge from the least-expected places. I was meeting with a Kuwaiti investor who remarked, "I like your private equity transactions because you use my money to buy a company, and three or four years later you sell it and we get the profits from the sale. [Three to five years is the typical life span of a private equity investment.] But I would like something we could keep for many years that would throw off regular returns."

AlixPartners satisfied that need. AlixPartners is a well-established, highly regarded global advisory firm. Like our Kuwaiti investor, Jay Alix, its founder, was looking for long-term investors who wouldn't shunt it off every three to five years.

Investcorp knew AlixPartners well because Dave Tayeh, now Investcorp's head of Private Equity North America, had served as chairman of the board of AlixPartners. Like Investcorp, Alix was known for building a deep relationship with the organizations it advised. Our two firms shared a philosophy that such partnerships were a marriage, not a fling. Then, too, Alix's consulting services could create strong synergies with Investcorp's portfolio companies.

Coming off the 3i acquisition, Investcorp couldn't afford to buy AlixPartners. It was too big a piece for us to swallow; and anyway, Alix-Partners was looking to sell only a portion, not the entire company. (The management of AlixPartners remains the largest shareholder.) Instead, Investcorp formed a consortium of institutional investors.

The transaction marked the first time Investcorp partnered with a major pension fund on a deal. It was the first time Investcorp committed to hold an investment for ten years, which was highly unusual for us. And it was the first time that Investcorp agreed to take a minority stake in a business—up until then, Investcorp had almost always been the majority shareholder in its portfolio companies in the United States and Europe. In one fell swoop, three of Investcorp's fundamental operating methods were shattered. "It was an example of Mohammed pushing the envelope and saying, 'We need to do things differently,'" said Dave.

AlixPartners was valued overall at $2.5 billion, and deals this size reverberate through the marketplace. At that point, it was the largest company Investcorp had ever taken an equity stake in, even though Investcorp couldn't write the biggest check. Given AlixPartners's size and

With the late President
of the UAE, HH Sheikh
Zayed bin Sultan Al
Nahyan

With Sheikh Mohammed
bin Zayed bin Sultan Al
Nahyan, President of the
UAE and Ruler of Abu
Dhabi, and General David
H. Petraeus (US Army,
Ret.), a Partner at KKR
and Chairman of the KKR
Global Institute

With Charles, Prince of Wales,
now King of the United Kingdom

With His Majesty, the late Sultan
Qaboos of Oman

With HRH the Crown Prince and Prime Minister of Bahrain Salman bin Hamad Al Khalifa, and Prime Minister of the UK, the Rt. Hon. Rishi Sunak, during the official visit of the Bahrain delegation to the UK in 2023

With the late Colin Powell, former US Secretary of State

With the late Kofi Annan, former Secretary-General of the United Nations, in Investcorp's London office in 2016

With Edouard Philippe, Prime Minister of France, in 2018

With General Luhut Binsar Pandjaitan, Coordinating Minister of Maritime and Investment Affairs of Indonesia, and Yongky Oktavianto, Investcorp Relationship Manager, in 2019

With Sheikh Hasina, Prime Minister of Bangladesh, in 2019

With (from right) Jeremy Ghose, Tim Mattar, Firas El Amine, Thomas Wong, and Rishi Kapoor in Tokyo in 2019

With Pedro Sánchez, Prime Minister of Spain, in 2022

With Paul Chan, Financial Secretary of Hong Kong, in 2023

With HRH Salman bin Hamad Al Khalifa, the Crown Prince, Prime Minister, and Deputy Supreme Commander, Kingdom of Bahrain, 2016

In the cockpit of a Jaguar fighter bomber, 2002

Tokyo office opening, February 2023

GCC Roadshow in Kuwait, March 2020

GCC Roadshow in March 2022 in Riyadh with (from left) Firas El Amine, Hazem Ben-Gacem, Mohammed Alardhi (center), Yusef Al Yusef, Yasser Bajsair and Nahar Houthan

Visiting FreshToHome's processing plant in India in 2021

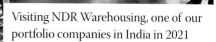

Visiting NDR Warehousing, one of our portfolio companies in India in 2021

Visiting NDR Warehousing, one of our portfolio companies in India in 2021

Visiting the India office in Mumbai before the opening in 2019

During a town hall meeting in the India office

With Rishi Kapoor (to Mohammed Alardhi's right) during a visit to India in 2021

Planting a tree at a K-12 school in Gurugram, India, in 2021

Visit to a K-12 school in Gurugram, India, in 2021

Speaking at IMD Business School for Management and Leadership in October 2022

Speaking at Gurugram University in India in 2021

A typical travel schedule involves flying around the world at least once a year

Mohammed Alardhi as a child, with his father

Special moments with the family

Group photo at the Strategic Partners Conference in Paris in 2018

Group photo at the Alternatives Symposium in New York in 2022

Celebrating ringing the opening bell at NASDAQ in March 2022

Celebrating ringing the opening bell at NASDAQ in March 2022 with (from left) Pete Rommeney, Andrea Davis, Dave Tayeh, Laura Coquis, Hazem Ben-Gacem, Jon Dracos, Mohammed Alardhi, Fortune Chigwende, Rishi Kapoor, Elena Ranguelova, Firas El Amine and Jan Erik Back

Group photo at Real Estate event in Madrid in 2022

At the World Economic Forum in Davos, Switzerland, in 2022

Meeting of the Investcorp International Advisory Board in London in 2022. Seated (from left): Ana Palacio, Ann-Kristin Achleitner, Mohammed Alardhi, Frances Townsend and Sir Michael Fallon. Standing (from left): Deepak Parekh, Urds Rohner, Heizo Takenaka, Ute Geipel-Faber, Mohamed El-Erian and Frederick Ma Si-Hang

With former United States Secretary of State Mike Pompeo in New York in 2023

University of Oxford England, in 2016

INSEAD, France, in 2018

IMD Business School for Management and Leadership, Switzerland, in 2019

ESMT (European School of Management and Technology), Berlin, in 2023

OpCom Offsite, Austria, in 2017

Group photo at OpCom Offsite, Greece, in 2018

2018 OpCom Offsite, Greece

OpCom Offsite, Portugal, in 2019

OpCom Offsite, New York, in 2022

OpCom Offsite, New York, in 2023

Mumbai office opening, in January 2019

Singapore office opening,
in March 2022

DOORS OF OMAN

This poster reminds people that our
business is about opening doors to new
opportunities

A poster illustrating our people working
from home during the COVID lockdown,
2020

scope, the transaction raised Investcorp's profile significantly, both in the United States and globally.

AN EMERGING MARKET ON OUR DOORSTEP

At the same time, our efforts to create a line of business that invested Middle Eastern money *in* the Middle East were beginning to bear fruit. The first Gulf Opportunity Fund had been founded under Nemir's leadership to attract financial institutions in the region, especially sovereign wealth funds, that don't commit to a deal-by-deal model. That first offering had been capitalized at over $1 billion in 2007, but owing to the nature of private businesses in the Gulf, it took a long time and a lot of work to build a promising portfolio.

The region was, essentially, an emerging market, explained Walid Majdalani, who leads our team there, with all the challenges and growing pains you might expect—and many that were surprises. (The Gulf Opportunity Fund II never actually launched. Instead, it evolved into two subsequent vehicles. The Abrdn Global Infrastructure Income Fund, a joint venture with Aberdeen Standard, now rebranded abrdn, launched in 2020 and is primarily focused on infrastructure projects in Saudi Arabia. We're presently raising capital for a fund aimed at helping family businesses in Saudi Arabia make the necessary adjustments to become public companies.)

Now that work was finally paying off. We bought a 25 percent stake in Fitness Time, which operated health clubs for men in Saudi Arabia. We really wanted to open women-only health clubs, but Saudi rules at the time stipulated that women could access gyms only if they were affiliated with a medical facility and, therefore, used primarily for physical rehabilitation. However, we kept our eyes open, and as soon as the rules changed, we quickly identified four or five women-only facilities we could immediately turn into a chain we called Fitness Ladies. We had the first-mover advantage, and eventually we offered gyms aimed at different market segments, including facilities that were more hardcore, more relaxed, focused on youth, and so on. The parent company became the largest operator of fitness clubs in the region, and we later successfully listed it on the Saudi Stock Exchange (Tadawul).

We also invested in the $2.5 billion Bindawood chain of supermarkets and hypermarkets in Saudi Arabia, which further promoted Investcorp's prominence in the Gulf's financial markets. And in 2016, we led the IPO for L'azurde, the fourth-largest gold manufacturer in the world and the first private equity–sponsored company to be listed on the Saudi Stock Exchange.

The message was that Investcorp was venturing into new products and new geographies. These examples gave us the confidence and the strength to take more risks. And the success of these ventures encouraged the firm to look into different markets, such as our subsequent moves into India and Asia, which I describe in chapter 7.

LIVING THE VISION

The agreement to acquire 3i's debt management business was announced on October 25, 2016. (It would close in the first half of 2017.) The agreement to acquire ownership stakes in AlixPartners was announced just two weeks later. We were knocking out milestone deals of the sort we had never done before.

That November, Yusef Al Yusef, who is now the head of Investcorp's private wealth platform in the Gulf, was attending the annual investors' conference in Abu Dhabi—the same conference at which, a year earlier, investors had applauded my announcement of the goal of $25 billion AUM. Now, a year later, our AUM was nudging $23 billion.

Yusef was about to get a big surprise.

Yusef later told me, "I turned on the television that morning and learned that the evening before, at the inaugural dinner of the conference, you had announced a new goal of $50 billion AUM. At the conference, I had a couple of Gulf investors at my table. They asked, 'Are you serious? $50 billion?' We hadn't reached $25 billion AUM yet."

But I was confident we could do it.

"We were becoming more open to adapting our business model, even if it meant departing from our previous practices," observed Abdul Rahim Saad, now the head of Global Partnerships. "People began to realize we could augment our historical practice without undermining it. We could complement, not substitute. It was a tectonic shift, functionally and culturally."

Hazem Ben-Gacem put it slightly differently: "We were living the vision articulated at the 2015 meeting at The Grove. There was a sense that the future was *now*."

CHAPTER 7

MAKE YOUR OWN LUCK

I believe you can make your own luck. The saying goes that "Luck is what happens when preparation meets opportunity." I believe that if you do the right things and are in the right places, opportunities will open up. However, it's what you do with those opportunities—how prepared you are and whether you have what you need to maximize that luck—that will determine the return on your investment.

By 2018, most of the heavy lifting had been done; we'd followed the road map sketched out three years earlier. "From then on," said co-CEO Rishi Kapoor, "it was a case of 'Let's grow.'"

The firm had blasted through its initial target of $25 billion in AUM in 2017. Each additional billion represented more doors being opened, more confidence in breaking the status quo, and more audacity in exploring new geographies, new asset classes, and new investors and partners.

The road map introduced in 2015 still shaped our fundamental strategy, but now we layered on a long-range plan, or LRP. Every six months or so, we would examine and update the road map to reflect changing market conditions and our own evolving capabilities, and consequently we would determine a new AUM goal.

Now, we set a new goal: $50 billion in AUM. Getting to $50 billion would require the firm to broaden its investment horizons even further—

among both investors and in the opportunities in which they could place their money.

As mentioned earlier, you can expand both organically and inorganically, through partnerships and through new markets. When we were doing things entirely organically, as we'd done historically, we settled at about $10 billion AUM. Since 2015, however, we had opened up the idea of acquiring new businesses and capabilities inorganically, and we embedded them inside Investcorp so they would become native to Investcorp. Much as we did during the first leg of the journey, we would need to make that happen on a continued—and even greater—basis for the next leg.

Over the next three years (2017–2019), Investcorp expanded the road map into adjacent spaces, opening new markets in new geographies, tapping new sources of capital, and forging relationships with a new type of investor.

OPENING NEW MARKETS: INDIA

In April 2017, Investcorp opened an office in Singapore. The credit management team already had a presence in Singapore; their local knowledge had established a beachhead for us to expand operations in Asia and served as a platform from which we could now analyze investment trends in the region.

One geography we were eyeing with particular interest was India. India is among the five largest economies in the world. You can't be a globally diversified alternative investments–focused manager without a strategy that includes India. But for a long time we didn't have one. India seemed too tough, too risky, too foreign, and not material for our business. But that didn't mean we ignored it.

Throughout 2017, Investcorp explored the landscape of financial investing in India: market sectors, government policies, the direction of the economy. We analyzed the demographic trends of the world's second-largest population. (As I write this in 2023, India is about to take over the top spot from China.) We found that, based on urbanization levels, India appeared today to be where China was in 2000, with cities contributing 75 percent of the country's GDP, driven by a young and growing middle class. Between urbanization and the government's recent pro-growth initiatives, we concluded that there were attractive opportunities over the medium to long term in housing, consumer tech, healthcare, and financial services—all areas we were familiar with.

We invited Deepak Parekh, a prominent banker who helped develop India's financial sector, to join our International Advisory Board. He, in turn, introduced Investcorp to IDFC Alternatives, a Mumbai-based company that was open to spinning off and selling its investment management and real estate businesses.

"As we thought about our own potential market in India, this seemed a thoughtful way to enter," Rishi recalled. "We wouldn't have to assemble a whole team from scratch, which can be hit or miss. We certainly were not going to commit the cardinal sin of flying in a bunch of people from New York or Bahrain, and thinking they could understand the market. The Indians already had well-established connections and had assets under management."

However, remember that for the first thirty-three years of Investcorp's existence, the firm had never done a single strategic corporate acquisition. We had dipped our toe in the water with a very small acquisition in our U.S. hedge funds business. Then, in 2016–2017, we purchased 3i's debt management business, which was a very big deal. At the time, we didn't know whether the 3i acquisition would be a one-time transaction. Looking forward, though, it was clear that inorganic growth through acquisitions would be a major engine driving us to our goal of $50 billion AUM. We had to learn to do it right.

IDFC would become the template for inorganic growth through an integrated acquisition.

MAKING A GOOD MATCH

Why were we interested in IDFC as opposed to one of its peers? Let's take a quick detour to discuss what kind of businesses are a good fit for Investcorp.

There's an easy way to assess whether a business enhances our portfolio. First, we evaluate whether the business will provide us with access to a new set of capabilities, through some combination of product, market, or asset class; or whether it will help scale up an existing line of business. Second, the business has to come with an existing investor base that complements our own investor universe. Third, there has to be an opportunity to cross-sell: their products should appeal to our clients and our products should appeal to theirs. With these three primary considerations, we can determine what a good fit should be.

But, of course, there's more to a compatible match than simply looking good on paper.

What we've come to realize is that the difference between the strategic acquisitions that succeed and those that disappoint is whether there's a good cultural fit. Of course, we do comprehensive financial due diligence, but behind all the quantitative analyses and the numbers are flesh-and-blood people. They are the x-factor in every equation.

We can hire individual employees and expect them to integrate with the culture of our firm. But when we bring on a group of employees who have operated as a team under a different umbrella, they behave differently from how they would if we hired them individually. Spending time with them up front gives us a sense of whether the people—not just the business—will fit into Investcorp.

"We all get what's called 'deal lust,' when you just want to complete the deal," said Rishi, who has led most of our strategic acquisitions. "But I would rather not do a corporate acquisition, even if it seems to stack up well on paper, if we're not comfortable with the people."

We do the same due diligence for a firm's cultural compatibility—or the lack of it—as we do for its financials. We spend a lot of time up front with the management team; that is, not just the company's founder or leaders but, rather, the people who will drive the company forward.

When making an "acquihire"—the term for buying a company primarily for the skills and expertise of their people, rather than the products or services they supply—it's absolutely crucial to understand what motivates their people and shapes their behavior. What are the group dynamics? Do they shift depending on who's participating in a meeting and whether it's a one-on-one conversation or a group meeting? How healthy are the relationships that drive the business?

We want to understand how the company has built their business. Are they ambitious? Do they deliver on their promises? How do they lead their organization? Do the behaviors they exhibit when you engage with them align with your own behaviors and thinking? As we extend our due diligence to connect with their market, we consider how they deal with people externally as well as internally.

These assessments are admittedly difficult to quantify, especially for hard-nosed financial folks. We're going with our gut and trying to evaluate something amorphous, rather than calculating facts and figures. But this is such a people business, particularly in the private-markets world where we live and operate. There is no shortage of capital. But there is always a shortage of high-quality human beings.

That's not just the big thing, it's the main thing.

Despite doing due diligence to the *n*th degree, in a people business there's a key element of trust that we both *have* to rely on. We are engaging with people whom we trust to keep their word—and they are trusting us. Otherwise, we wouldn't be able to get anything done.

After we decide to go forward, another key to a successful acquihire is planting "culture carriers" from Investcorp inside the target organization. We learned that capability when we acquired 3i's credit business. Initially, we didn't have Investcorp people within that group. But we started integrating their people to our teams, first in our distribution team, then in finance and legal. That gave them a new home that was truly part of Investcorp.

Most culture gets disseminated and absorbed through osmosis, so a win is all about creating an environment that's conducive to osmosis. If we have an entire team coming into our organization, the members of that team naturally default to sticking together instead of opening up. That can lead to "organ rejection," an "us versus them" perspective that's always the kiss of death.

Consequently, our corporate acquisition playbook is centered on driving four elements of cultural compatibility: ensuring that the people coming across are comfortable with Investcorp before the deal is finalized; using that initial interaction to evaluate whether the deal is right in the first place, when it is still possible to decline instead of having to eventually divorce; facilitating integration through culture carriers; and recognizing that our way is not always the only way.

We used to have a tendency to assume that the administrative operations of whatever company we had acquired would have to fit into our corporate infrastructure. One of the things we've come to appreciate is that our way is *not* always better. If the setup of their IT and HR functions is better for them, if their outsourcing decisions make sense, we don't try to fix something that isn't broken.

HITTING THE GROUND RUNNING

IDFC Alternatives checked all the necessary boxes, plus one very big box I hadn't mentioned earlier: they were available and willing. There were not many home-grown private equity platforms in India, as opposed to external private equity firms that had swooped in and done deals with Indian companies. We wanted to nurture and grow local talent that could leverage its own local network.

This is always the challenge when you're looking to land an acquisition: you decide which pool you want to fish in, cast your line (through investment banks or contacts, like Deepak Parekh), and hope to get some bites. However, there aren't always a lot of fish in the pond, and they may not be interested in what you're offering. We were lucky. Not only did IDFC bite but they were exactly what we were looking for.

In January 2019, Investcorp bought IDFC Alternatives's private equity and real estate investment businesses, two asset classes primary to Investcorp's DNA. With this acquihire, Rishi said, "We hit the ground running."

What we did with IDFC was almost the reverse of what we had done with 3i's credit management business. With 3i, we bought a large company; with IDFC, we bought a small one. We said, "We can take this small platform and with the resources we have at Investcorp, we can ensure that we build it out before it gets too developed and set in its ways."

IDFC was a 100 percent Indian team, very much focused on the domestic Indian market and with no global experience per se. Their investors and capital came primarily from the domestic Indian market. Being acquired by Investcorp gave them access to a much larger pool of investors from around the world, which could bring them additional capital. In addition, they would be part of an asset management firm with over thirty-five years' experience in both private equity and real estate, which was looking to leverage that heritage in the Indian market.

All that added up: international investors, plus an understanding parent who wanted to grow the business and had a level of experience that IDFC didn't have. These factors made a compelling argument for being acquired by us. The global element—how Investcorp could connect the dots around the world—appealed to them as well. And as I describe in chapter 9, that's exactly what we did, helping domestic Indian businesses like FreshToHome and NephroPlus expand not just within India but to other countries as well.

The IDFC acquisition was the perfect opportunity to experiment with the concept of a dedicated "culture carrier." (With 3i, we had known and worked closely with Jeremy Ghose and his management team for years, so we didn't need one.) The guy we identified for this had checked all the boxes: Harsh Shethia had spent over fifteen years at Investcorp, was of Indian origin, had studied in the United States, and had worked at Goldman Sachs before coming to us. Harsh embodied all the dimensions of the Investcorp profile, as well; he was steeped in the culture of the firm in terms of mindset, client outlook, performance, and unquestioned integrity. We asked him to take on the role of "managing partner," a new position we created.

One year after we acquired the IDFC business, the COVID-19 pandemic hit and the world went into lockdown. Fortunately, Harsh was already in situ, fully integrated into IDFC. Had he not been there, we would have had real problems. The team would have had difficulty being an outpost on their own and COVID would have made them even more isolated. Instead, they continued to invest throughout COVID and did brilliantly.

Rishi said, "You may enter a space through an acquisition, but if you do a good job integrating the acquisition, with the passage of time that capability becomes native. Now we think of Investcorp as having been in India not for two years but for twenty, because the team's experience investing in that market spans two decades."

We feel the same way about 3i's credit management business.

At Investcorp, there is a tradition of recognizing a person's years at the firm. There's a ceremony at which we publicly celebrate people's commitment with a long-service certificate. Jeremy Ghose still marvels at being awarded a thirty-year certificate. He said, "3i had been part of Investcorp for only three years at the time, but Mohammed recognized that I had been part of the credit management entity for thirty years. That blew me away."

OPENING NEW MARKETS: CHINA

Like India, China is important to our growth journey. It's the world's second-largest economy and it accounted for the largest share of global GDP growth in the past decade (followed by India and the U.S.).[1]

For most people outside Asia, China is its own universe. "Although it has rapidly become more westernized, its language and culture are very different," explained co-CEO Hazem Ben-Gacem, who spearheaded our China strategy. "And the subtext—you hear all these stories about 'Communist China'—doesn't help."

Investcorp had been indirectly investing in China through our portfolio companies for years. For example, Leica Geosystems, one of our most successful investments, had its main manufacturing business located in China.

With our India strategy well underway, we sharpened our focus on China. In 2018, Hazem and I went on a fact-finding mission to Hong Kong and the mainland. We spoke to bankers and accountants, and friends and family, to hear what they had to say about everything from the rule of law to how people have made or lost money, to what the challenges might be. After that trip, Hazem spent a lot of time in Hong Kong "getting educated," as he put it.

It's been said that in India you invest with the private sector, while in China you invest with the government. That's how our approach was executed. We came across China Everbright, a Hong Kong–based SOE—a state-owned enterprise created by the government to partake in commercial activities on the government's behalf—that, like us, was an alternative asset manager.

At the time, there were about 120 SOEs in China. Everbright was looking to launch a fund specializing in high-growth new technology. That's a field we know very well; our due diligence showed that China has the world's highest number of internet users and is home to some of the fastest-growing "unicorn" technology companies, companies that reach a valuation of $1 billion without being listed on the stock market. Everbright seemed like a promising partner to introduce us to this new market.

For its part, Everbright was looking for a source of additional capital. When you talk about private markets in China, that means foreign investment. If you take one step back, you find that institutional capital had been streaming into China for quite a while, channeled particularly into public equities. Take two steps back, and you'll find that the influx of institutional capital, in turn, had been influenced by a number of bigger private equity players who had gone into China well before we decided to make our move.

We could bring something different, however. For years, many of the Gulf family businesses that were our clients had been asking us to bring them investment opportunities in China. We had been the bridge between private wealth in the Gulf and investments in the West. Now we could be the bridge for Middle Eastern capital to flow into China. An SOE was both familiar territory for us and less risky than some alternatives. In September 2018, we took a substantial stake in the Everbright Limited New Economy Fund. That was the debut of our business in China.

If India provided a master class in inorganic growth through a buy-and-build approach, our strategy in China was a more hybrid but no less successful lesson. Our partnership with Everbright soon expanded, as we assembled our own investment team and, in November 2019, we combined the two to jointly manage the China Everbright New Economy Fund I. A year later, we opened our office in Beijing.

"Our experience has been terrific," reported Hazem, whose business card lists his name and title in English and Chinese. "There's a lot of similarity to the Gulf countries, where you have a central leadership passionately focused on growth and on leveraging external capital. There's a similar business mindset and culture. You no sooner leave a dinner meeting then the emails start flying."

As we always do, we have focused on the macro trends to find promising investment opportunities. The biggest issue facing China today is an aging population, with 1.4 billion people who need access to services. With the number of people over sixty projected to constitute 28 percent of the total population by 2040,[2] China will need more services related to healthcare. At the same time, thanks to the country's ongoing economic transformation, a potential 120 million households are set to become middle-class consumers in the next decade.[3] That, in turn, is driving demand for access to technology and consumer services. These are three sectors that are sweet spots for Investcorp.

Similar trends are emerging throughout Southeast Asia. "Southeast Asia is a bloc that's bigger than Western Europe and the United States put together, so it's a natural place for us to explore," Hazem said. "The energy and momentum remind me of London thirty years ago."

One of our most exciting investment platforms these days is the Asia Food Growth Fund, which focuses on branded condiments, packaged foods, and healthy snacks in the region's highly fragmented food sector. Our colleagues ate a lot of ramen as part of their research, and I'm happy to say that it's paying off.

TAPPING NEW SOURCES OF CAPITAL

Although Investcorp had a global mindset from its inception, as I've said, the capital for our investments primarily came from the Gulf. Even as our investments became more global, the capital stayed local. "One of the changes since 2015 was to ask ourselves, 'How do we start building a more global investor base?'" recalled Tim Mattar.

Diversifying our sources of capital became a significant issue as I was preparing to become Executive Chairman, owing to fluctuating oil prices. After peaking at nearly $108 per barrel in June 2014, petroleum prices plummeted to just over $44 per barrel in January 2015, a drop of nearly 60 percent in a little over seven months.[4] The price would drop even further before bottoming out in early 2016, marking one of the three biggest declines since World War II.[5]

The collapse of oil prices affected our investors in a big way. When oil prices drop, the economies of the Gulf get hammered. Governments then don't spend as much, so a lot of business activities that depend on government spending face economic turmoil. Our investors don't make as much money, so they don't invest as much.

Investcorp was so closely identified with the Gulf that our fortunes were assumed to mirror the economies of the Gulf Cooperation Council, or GCC, the political and economic alliance of six nations in the region. (GCC members include Bahrain, Kuwait, Oman, Qatar, Saudi Arabia, and the United Arab Emirates.) Any fluctuation in the price of oil had a ripple effect that hit us, too.

Year after year, when the international ratings agencies came to assess the firm, one of their top priorities was evaluating how oil prices would impact our plans to raise capital. If oil prices were down, there would be always some doubt about whether we could execute our business plan for the coming year. In 2015, our base investors were hurting, but they were still supporting us. So, there was a lot of pressure on us to deliver on our vision.

Mubadala's investment in us came at a critical time and helped renew our investors' trust and confidence. It was the right time to announce, "Investcorp is evolving. We are going to scale up our businesses in the U.S. and Europe. For the first time, we will be exploring opportunities in Asia, building a presence in India, and starting the process in China. As a result, we will be able to provide our investors with a broader range of opportunities to deploy capital with us."

I think that statement reassured investors that they could continue to give us their money but get returns from a variety of options around the globe, as opposed to just one or two products. At the same time, it was clear we needed to dilute our concentration risk in an area of the world that was little understood by external parties, not by reducing our business in the Gulf but, rather, by tapping additional sources of capital.

A significant step in this new direction was taking a minority stake in United Talent Agency (UTA), a fast-growing Los Angeles–based talent and entertainment company that was the third-largest talent agency in the world. It was the first time that 100 percent of Investcorp's capital was raised in the United States.

Equally significant was that this was the first time we joined forces exclusively with Western, rather than Gulf, institutional investors—insurance companies, another alternative asset manager, and a Canadian pension fund—rather than relying solely on individual investors.

A key element in our vision of growth was to move in a large way to attract institutional capital. Institutional investors are organizations that invest on behalf of others: pension funds, banks, sovereign wealth funds, mutual funds, hedge funds, endowments, and insurance companies. Institutional capital is sustainable and long term. It's not affected by fluctuations in oil prices (unless, of course, it's a sovereign wealth fund from a petro power). And there's a lot of it in the world. The collapse in oil prices made it more natural for us and our investors and stakeholders to understand our shift in strategy. (We knew that to attract institutional money we needed the right products. I describe this strategy in more detail in chapter 8.)

By the way, Investcorp sold its stake in UTA in 2022, after the company more than tripled its EBITDA (earnings before interest, tax, depreciation, and amortization) in four years.

SEEDING STRATEGIC RELATIONSHIPS

In February 2018, I attended a dinner hosted by oil giant Aramco, at the Davos World Economic Forum. I exchanged my name and affiliation with the very British gentleman seated next to me: "I'm Mohammed Alardhi. I'm the executive chairman of an investment firm called Investcorp."

He replied, "I'm Gerry Grimstone. I'm the chairman of Barclay's and Aberdeen Standard." Then we settled down to chat.

Chemistry is a big part of doing business. In a classic case of serendipity, we discovered we had much in common: Gerry had worked in the Ministry of Defence, I had a military background. We were both interested in investing in infrastructure projects. We got on very well. We decided to meet up in London with our respective CEOs to brainstorm ways in which we could work together.

Aberdeen Standard (now called abrdn) was—and is—one of the largest asset managers in the U.K., with a specialty in investing in social infrastructure, such as healthcare, education, housing, and the building blocks of smart cities. Investcorp, of course, knew the Gulf inside and out. We recognized the region has a fast-growing population and that governments were taking steps to diversify their economies away from oil, and were prioritizing investment in social infrastructure. Combining our two strengths made sense.

A year after the Davos meeting, in February 2019, Investcorp and Aberdeen announced a joint venture targeting critical social infrastructure in the GCC. This, in turn, would lead two years later to the launch of a regional investment fund to invest in GCC infrastructure. Confirming Investcorp's rising status, Saudi Arabia's Public Investment Fund (PIF), one of the largest sovereign wealth funds in the world, committed to be an anchor investor, in addition to a substantial commitment from the Beijing-based Asian Infrastructure Investment Bank (AIIB), another high-profile, top-notch institution.

A month earlier, in January 2019, Investcorp had entered a milestone relationship with Coller Capital in the private equity secondaries market. Here's what that means: When Investcorp's investors give the firm their money to buy a particular company, they commit that money for a certain period of time—usually four to five years—with the assumption that at the end of that time Investcorp will sell the company at a profit and return their original capital with a nice profit. But what if the company is doing so well that it could continue to grow? Why get rid of the goose when it still has the potential to lay plenty of golden eggs, just because the terms of the agreement stipulated that you would own the goose only for five years?

That's where the private equity secondaries market comes in. If investors give their permission, Investcorp will transfer the ownership of the goose to companies like Coller. Then Coller assumes the risk while Investcorp continues to manage the company. Under its management, the goose continues to lay its golden eggs, which makes everyone happy.

That's what Investcorp did with Dainese, an Italian manufacturer of stylish protective gear for motorcyclists. Investcorp bought Dainese from its founder; after reaching maturity four years later, the investment had tripled in value. But the feeling was that there was still much more potential to tap. So, with the permission of the original investors, Investcorp essentially transferred Dainese, along with five or six of our other assets, into a quasi-fund created for that specific purpose, of which Coller bought a majority share. We continued to manage the companies in what we now called "the Coller fund." (Coller referred to it as "the Investcorp fund.") Our investors had the option of staying in the Coller fund or being bought out at an agreed price. Those that chose to stay put reaped a very nice reward.

Three years later, the investment had indeed doubled. In other words, rather than "only" tripling the investment in four years, by extending the period to seven years through a relationship with a secondary funder, the investment sextupled when it was sold to The Carlyle Group, another private equity firm.

The deal with Coller was a strategic milestone, for two reasons. First, Coller committed roughly $1 billion, two-thirds of which was allocated for secondary transactions like Dainese and one-third of which was given to Investcorp to invest in future deals. That was a big step in contributing to Investcorp's target of reaching $50 billion AUM in the medium term. Second, Coller is one of the largest private equity secondary players in the world.

"They have a great reputation in the market," explained Daniel Lopez-Cruz, who, as then-head of our European Private Equity group, was very involved in the U.K.-based Coller deal. "They weren't going to invest $1 billion in companies managed by just anybody. They needed to have confidence in both the investment *and* the investment team."

When you work with institutional investors, you're truly playing in the big leagues, on a global scale. They're not a single investor or a wealthy family office. The size of the Coller deal was the seal of approval that would launch Investcorp's push to attract institutional investors around the world.

BULKING UP THE BRAIN TRUST

During this period, Investcorp not only reached out to embrace new opportunities but also looked inward to reexamine and strengthen its brain trust.

The most elemental change involved the Board of Directors. Since the firm's inception, the seventeen-person board had been composed exclusively of members from GCC countries. The board was a who's who of merchant families from the Gulf, carefully chosen by Nemir Kirdar, whose names automatically conferred blue-chip credibility in the region. However, as Investcorp became more global, there was a need to add new blood, new expertise, and critically, an international dimension to the board.

We now reduced the board to a more manageable twelve members and broadened its purview. (The board was expanded to fourteen in 2022.) The aim was to build a board with the ability to ask probing questions, as Investcorp ventured into new industries, and to leverage their knowledge to eliminate blind spots.

Among the six new members elected to the board in 2019 were Gregory So, the former Secretary for Commerce and Economic Development for Hong Kong, who was plugged into China; Joachim Faber, the founding CEO of Allianz Global Investors, which under his leadership had acquired bond-fund giant PIMCO; and Gerry Grimstone. (Sir Gerry stepped down when he was asked to become the U.K.'s Minister of Investment under then-Prime Minister Boris Johnson.) In addition, there were two new members, both of whom came from Saudi Arabia, the largest country in the GCC and the GCC country with the greatest potential for the critical social infrastructure development that Investcorp targeted for its future growth: Abdullatif Al Othman, the ex-CFO of Aramco and the owner of a Saudi-based engineering consultancy; and Mazen Fakeeh, whose background as a medical doctor (whose family had built hospitals and medical schools) aligned with Investcorp's plans to focus on healthcare-related transactions.

Now we had the different backgrounds and skills we needed around one table. But there was still one significant gap in our leadership. That was remedied in January 2021, when Frances Townsend was appointed to the Board of Directors. Fran was already a member of our International Advisory Board (which I describe later), where as the former Homeland Security Advisor to President George W. Bush she brought valuable knowledge of international policy and governance issues, both in the United States and in the Middle East. In addition to her unquestioned expertise, Fran's presence signaled Investcorp's commitment to developing and promoting talented women. Diversity at the highest levels is something we were going to need more of, both to attract top female talent and to demonstrate to the world that our vision was truly global and that we were ready for prime time.

There were equally consequential shifts in the International Advisory Board. The concept of an advisory board originated with Nemir Kirdar in the 1990s. The idea was that in those geographies where we don't have offices, but we do have a big investment presence, we should have "ambassadors" to inform us about that region. Under Nemir's aegis, however, the spotlight was limited to Europe—in fact, the board was called the "European Advisory Board." Now, the board became international.

The International Advisory Board is composed of wise men and women from different regions and walks of life. They don't have any responsibility to the firm, but when we gather together we tell them what we're doing and they give us their input. Mohamed El-Erian, the former CEO of PIMCO, could tell us what global economies are doing and the implications of governmental policies on business. Frances Townsend brought more than twenty-five years of international policy-making, as well as legal and business strategy experience. Ann-Kristin Achleitner was (and is) a high-profile researcher in the field of entrepreneurial finance, with a particular focus on social entrepreneurship and financing for social enterprises, both of which tied into Investcorp's policies concerning Environmental, Social, and Governance (ESG) issues. Among its other members, the board also included Sir Michael Fallon, the U.K.'s former Minister for Business and Secretary of Defence.

"Everyone is there for a reason," said Fran Townsend. "This is not 'The Mohammed Show.' He has a very clear goal of what he wants to pull from each of us and how he wants us to educate everyone else."

The International Advisory Board helps steer our strategy by offering guidance in everything we do, whether it's strategy or vision, as well as challenging us with different ideas and providing knowledge about things we may have missed in our due diligence about a particular country or sector. It gives us a behind-the-scenes picture we wouldn't see otherwise.

"It's all about blind spots," noted Tim Mattar. "We all have them—as individuals, as institutions, and as organizations—so you want to minimize them as much as possible. These are holistic views, rather than specific points, but they help us adjust our risk framework and steer our direction of travel."

The International Advisory Board meets once a year, as well as gathering at regional meetings and Investcorp advisory conferences, but members are welcome to weigh in at any time. So, for example, in January 2020, Mohamed El-Erian raised a red flag about a respiratory virus in China. "This is not a normal virus," he warned. "This is a shock. It will *not* be a depression. It will be like falling off a cliff."

Ann-Kristin Achleitner recalled, "We discussed the possibility of an economic crash—exactly of the kind we then had—just before COVID hit. To talk about risk doesn't mean you can predict the future. But it does mean that you can plan for it."

You can never be prepared for a pandemic, but at least we had some advance warning, so we could prepare how to react. COVID *was* like falling off a cliff, Ann-Kristin agreed, but thanks to the early alert, "at Investcorp, it was like falling off a cliff with a parachute." (I describe how Investcorp reacted to the COVID pandemic in chapter 10.)

Ann-Kristin has served on the board since 2018. She epitomizes the broad scope of influence of the International Advisory Board when she says, "I think most of the work I do is outside of the boardroom, not in the sessions." She served as a sounding board when we created and sponsored the Investcorp European Acquisition Corp. I, which marked our entry into the SPAC (special purpose acquisition companies) market. Like other board members, she draws on her experience in serving as a board member at other companies. "The challenges aren't always the same, but they can be analogous," she pointed out. "The big challenge is to see the analogy. It doesn't have to be someone from the same industry who can see it. And that's where the International Advisory Board can add value."

As we build our muscles to lift heavier weights and train to acquire different skills, the members of the International Advisory Board are a key element of our coaching team. "That's what you should do if you're on an advisory board," Ann-Kristin said. "You should be there for advice."

The learning doesn't stop there. "Since Mohammed became Executive Chairman, we've expanded the list of people in government, industry, and financial services we have access to," said Jon Dracos, whether it's in the context of inviting speakers for OpCom and investor conferences or internal town halls. "Having Mohamed El-Erian or David Rubenstein [Chairman of the Council on Foreign Relations and co-founder of The Carlyle Group] or Bob Gates [the U.S. Secretary of Defense under both George W. Bush and Barack Obama] come to your session to talk—that was a pretty different step up in class. Michael Milken spoke at one of our conferences. We had a dinner in Washington, D.C., with a group of ambassadors. For one of our town halls, I interviewed Frances Townsend about the situation in Russia—this was about four months before the invasion of Ukraine.

"That type of brain candy is new," Jon pointed out. "It's critical to our reputation in the marketplace. People say, 'Wow, that was an interesting speaker." And it enriches our pipeline by having access to people from outside our world who have fresh ideas and can help us think differently."

Nor is it limited to senior staff. "Engaging people in your group has been pushed to top of mind," Jon continued. "Town halls and monthly lectures are relatively new things that are pulling in a different level of personnel. We're still a work in progress on that, but we've come a long way."

"WE DON'T WANT TO BE JUST
ANOTHER LARGE-CAP PLAYER"

The firm's ability to successfully extend and expand its capabilities into new geographies, industries, and adjacent asset classes testified to our solid core capabilities. But incremental growth, while a viable strategy, wouldn't be enough to achieve the $50 billion AUM target.

"It's hard to rely on startups to get to $50 billion," Jon explained. "You have to stake established platforms and triple them in size. Mohammed pushed the idea of making big businesses bigger."

However, Investcorp faced a major hurdle in that approach. "One of the frustrations was that the size of our transactions was limited by our fundraising capacity," noted Yusef Al Yusef, who oversees the raising of capital in the Gulf. "We were stuck at the lower end of the mid-market category. The mid-market space is quite wide—a mid-market enterprise could be worth $200 million, or it could be worth $900 million. We don't want to be just another large-cap player. We want to be the leading alternative investment manager in the mid-cap space. But to accomplish that, we need to do larger transactions."

To accomplish *that* meant accessing a whole new class of investors.

CHAPTER 8

A DIFFERENT RELATIONSHIP WITH DIFFERENT INVESTORS

I n September 2021, we announced a new goal for Investcorp, a goal even more audacious than the earlier targets of $25 billion AUM or $50 billion AUM. It was $100 billion AUM, in about seven years.

During the previous six years, we had doubled our AUM, then doubled it again, to nearly $40 billion. We could indulge in a quick pat on the back, but in the world of global money management, $40 billion is not big. Furthermore, Investcorp had reached that target by scaling up our presence in adjacent businesses and markets, and by doubling down on our core capabilities to deepen our mindshare with a global investor base. While this was good, it wasn't good enough. Hazem Ben-Gacem pointed out, "You don't add another $60 billion by doing the same things you're doing today."

For over thirty years, Investcorp had been powered by one massive engine: money from our private clients in the Gulf. But there was a fundamental flaw in this model: every time you sell a portfolio company or finalize a real estate deal, you're handing money back. So, the AUM is going in the wrong direction. The size of your balance sheet determines your ability to underwrite multiple large transactions. You have good profit margins, but you can't scale. "It's like flying a 747 with only two engines," said Yusef Al Yusef. "You can stay in the air, but you won't have much forward motion."

As we looked to our next target of $100 billion AUM, we didn't just need to turbocharge the original engines. We needed to add another engine—namely, a different source of capital.

THE WIND UNDER OUR WINGS

"You don't get to $100 billion unless you have different relationships with different investors," Jon Dracos pointed out. "That's the biggest thing." By "different investors," we didn't mean the high-net-worth individuals and families similar to our Gulf clients but in other parts of the world.

We meant an entirely new class of investor: institutional investors.

"Institutional investor" is a term referring to capital sourced from institutions rather than from individuals: sovereign wealth funds, pension funds, insurance funds, endowments, and family offices. They are particularly desirable clients because they commit large amounts of capital up front, and they pay management fees on a regular basis, rather than paying one-time transaction fees. This build-up of committed capital, as it's called, would be the wind under our wings on our journey to $100 billion AUM. Convincing institutional investors to place their money with us would elevate the firm to the big leagues.

But it wouldn't be easy.

F. Scott Fitzgerald famously wrote "the very rich . . . are different from you and me." Similarly, institutional investors differ from individual investors in a number of significant ways, ways that would require a radical shift in our standard operating procedures.

A DIFFERENT APPROACH

Institutions and individuals come at investing from opposite ends of the spectrum. The wealthy individuals and business families who were our core clients thrilled to the specific transactions that Investcorp offered, whether those were Gucci or Simmons Mattress Company. They liked to evaluate each deal through the lens of their own experience and make their own decisions about whether to buy in. Investcorp offered the opportunities, but it was up to investors to build their own portfolios, which was something the firm had always encouraged.

Institutional investors, conversely, place individual transactions significantly lower on their priority list. They invest in blind pool funds, whose portfolios represent the sum of their team's decision-making powers. (A blind pool fund, also known as a "blank-check fund," is exactly what it sounds like: a limited partnership managed by a general partner, or GP, that raises money from limited partners, or LPs, without specifying in which transaction it will be placed. A typical offering is a ten-year fund, with a five-year investment period and a five-year harvest period.) Consequently, institutional investors focus on the thinking that drives the deals: *your* strategy, *your* investing niche, the collective brainpower of *your* team, *your* experience, *your* track record, where and why you've succeeded or failed, and ultimately, how all those elements align with their own interests.

Since its inception, Investcorp had been transaction focused, another term for our deal-by-deal model. If we wanted to attract institutional investors, we would have to become portfolio focused and create appropriate fund vehicles. Furthermore, it would be up to us to create the portfolio, not the investor. That would be a major adjustment. (Just to provoke future possibilities, once institutions are satisfied with the performance of a fund, they often wish to dip into individual transactions in the fund—something called "co-investment." This could be a sweet spot for Investcorp, but first we would have to attract the institutions.)

A DIFFERENT PRODUCT

This different approach demands a different product, which calls for a whole new set of decisions. To begin with, when you consider raising your first fund, the key is determining the initial fund size. Do you start with $250 million, $500 million, $750 million, or even $1 billion? There are many factors that go into determining this amount, including the team's prior experience. Have they done $50 million transactions or $500 million ones? Typically, a fund will invest in ten deals over a four- to five-year time span. With an average $50 million transaction size, your fund can start at $500 million (the minimum size), provided you can find the investors to back you.

Each successive fund is expected to be 50 to 100 percent larger, so if Fund I starts at $500 million, Fund II can go up to $1 billion, Fund III to $1.5 billion, and so on. However, some of the very largest institutional investors—the ones you aspire to claim as your clients—will not even contemplate investing in a fund that is less than $2 billion. So, your strategy must acknowledge that it will take several years to build up to larger-fund vehicles.

A blind pool fund is just the starting point. Institutional investors expect more investment options, to warrant the time and effort involved in doing the due diligence of examining your strategy, team, and track record. They may be interested in a fund that targets technology, for example, or a regionally focused fund in India. They may want to co-invest in one of Investcorp's portfolio companies. (Co-investments arise when an individual deal is too large for a fund to acquire on its own, providing the investors in the fund the opportunity to "top up" their exposure to that particular investment.)

"There's so much potential for cross-pollination within the firm," concluded Laura Coquis, who heads up our institutional investing team. "But it takes time for the potential to be made tangible."

A DIFFERENT PROCESS

Institutional managers not only have a very different approach than individual investors to making investment decisions. They drill down to levels of detail not seen since the Spanish Inquisition. This is exemplified by the due diligence questionnaire (the DDQ), a list of questions designed to mitigate risk by delving into every aspect of how the money will be managed. (They either send you their list or you proactively prepare your own list.)

"The DDQ covers everything under the sun," explained Tim Mattar. "I've seen DDQs that are over 150 pages of single-spaced lines. It's a marathon."

The sharpest focus is on your track record. Did you achieve your returns by luck or by skill? What is your ratio of wins to losses? When you made X amount of money on a particular deal, how much value came from the nature of the asset and how much from a timely market uptick?

The questionnaire also asks how the investment team is structured, the background of each individual on the team, their age, their tenure, and how the team is compensated. This last question is significant because the investor wants to make sure the team is happy at the firm and won't jump ship. To ensure consistent leadership, institutional investors often insert a "key man" clause in their Limited Partner Agreement (LPA), stipulating that if more than one key person on the investment team leaves, the fund will cease further investments and commence a liquidation process.

A DIFFERENT TIME FRAME

Institutional investors work on a different schedule. Even though many of our private clients have been with us for two—and even three—generations, they are under no obligation to stay after their asset has been sold. Institutional investors, however, sign up for the long haul.

Institutional investors don't think in terms of months or years. They think in terms of decades. Because they're buying into your broad track record over time, and because the commitment is much more serious, it takes months and months before you get anywhere. You offer them an initial opportunity that a private client might leap at and they'll say, "Come back to us on your second opportunity and we'll see."

Their concern is understandable. They're buying an investment capability, so they want to know how and where you made your money. The ultimate question is always: Can you do it again? Is this repeatable? Answering that question to their satisfaction requires a longer time frame.

DIFFERENT RELATIONSHIPS

Investcorp is known for its high-touch, high-focus relationships with our private clients, noted Savio Tung, Investcorp's former CIO and now a Senior Advisor. "Our pitch was, 'Each transaction is a unique opportunity for you to invest. You can pass but someone else may come in, so if you don't hurry up, you may lose this chance.' Our investors in the Gulf like that. They like to be part of the investment experience and to exercise their judgment to cherry-pick investments. They want to hear the ups and downs, they like the access to unique opportunities we provide. There's some emotion involved."

But the high-touch, constant face-to-face communication is labor intensive. It's not scalable. And because it costs us more time, the client's fees will be higher.

Institutional clients look for good performance but also for low fees. They value efficiency more than face-to-face communications. As Savio said, "If you don't call to wish them happy birthday, they don't care."

DIFFERENT RISKS

Individual investors make their own decisions to commit to a transaction. An investor who puts $100,000 into one deal and $500,000 into another can either be spectacularly right or spectacularly wrong. But no matter the amount or the outcome, it's their choice—not Investcorp's.

Institutional investors assume the risk when they put money into a fund, but the responsibility for building and managing the fund is entirely up to Investcorp. That requires thinking about asset allocation and diversification within the fund to balance the highs and the lows, which in turn demands a different set of skills by the investment teams.

///////

These were all new ideas for us. For over thirty years, we had constructed our strategy from the opposite direction: from the perspective of private clients. We'd always done things a certain way and now would have to change. There were a lot of uncertainties and a lot of questions.

LEVERAGING SCALABILITY

Investcorp's original deal-by-deal model had worked for decades. Why deviate from it?

The most basic advantage of having institutional investors as clients wouldn't just be the larger pools of money at our disposal. It was also the potential for scalability.

The fundamental problem with Investcorp's historical transaction boutique model was that it didn't provide a predictable income stream for the company, while its operating costs were more or less fixed. It's the difference between collecting rent every month and selling a property for a potentially big but ultimately unreliable return. Also, the deal-by-deal model tied up a big portion of our capital: Investcorp would buy a company, hold it for up to five years, and then sell it. Because we underwrote every transaction ourselves, we just didn't have the balance sheet to take on more than a few major deals at once.

We couldn't scale up.

However, with an institutional model, we would raise the money first and then deploy it. When institutional investors committed their capital to a blind pool, Investcorp could use that money to make more deals. And because the pool would be bigger, the deals could be larger. At the end of the day, whether you do a $100 million transaction or a $500 million transaction, the transaction costs are similar. But either way you get operating leverage you can't get otherwise. That's one key advantage in scaling up.

Another bonus: The larger the fund, the greater the amount of management fees. If you have raised a $1 billion fund and the management fee is 2 percent per annum, you know you'll be paid $20 million in fees every year, regardless of what happens in the market.

"Institutional investors don't pay large fees," Tim noted. "This is a major area of focus, and the larger the ticket they write, the larger the fee reduction they expect. But they know the market benchmarks and want the investment teams to be motivated by the right incentives." So, while you can't charge institutional investors a higher percentage, you ultimately generate more fees because you're managing a larger amount of money.

That's what institutional investors provide: scale, size, and a steady stream of income.

LEARNING A DIFFERENT LANGUAGE

Investcorp already had established relationships with some of the top institutional investors in the GCC, but there is a lot of wealth held by institutions outside the Gulf—plenty more than by institutions within the Gulf. And while the firm had plucked different strands of institutional capital from outside the GCC to tie up the UTA deal, as well as some other transactions, our approach had been piecemeal: a win here, a win there. There was no consistent or comprehensive strategy to get on the radar screens of global institutional investors.

Once again, we were faced with a choice of build versus buy. We initially thought that if we could do retail investing, we could cross over to an institutional clientele—sort of like picking up Spanish after learning French. We were wrong. This was more like learning Arabic: an entirely new alphabet, with idiosyncratic grammatical rules and totally different pronunciation.

We realized we needed someone who understood institutional investors and who could speak their language. More than that, we needed someone who could educate our internal constituents about the processes we'd need to put into place to achieve our goals. Over the years, we had gotten inside the skin of our individual investors. Now, we needed to do the same thing with institutional clients.

It took us over a year, from our initial decision, to find the right person. In September 2021, we brought in Laura Coquis, a specialist in institutional capital formation and investor relations strategies for private markets, to lead our global institutional capital-raising team and help us change the perspective and practices we had honed over thirty-plus years.

It would be a big transition. We needed to provide a compelling offer in every dimension: a strong team, a reliable track record, a platform that made it easy for clients to work with us, as well as a full spectrum of products that would align with their investment style and goals.

Coming in as a new entrant in this field, we were very much behind the eight ball. Prospective investors would say—and rightly so—"You've been around for nearly forty years. Why are you raising Fund I now? Blackstone's Fund I was raised decades ago." Laura's answer was, "It isn't that we've come up short. It's that we're just starting the journey."

And, in fact, we had some real differentiators that very few other firms had. First, our Fund I was not our first-time fund. We had a four-decade pedigree in mid-market asset management that included a variety of funds in that space. "I don't think there's a firm that's been investing in the middle market of private equity and real estate for forty years with the fantastic track record, the stable organization, and the opportunity for partnership that we can offer," said Laura. "Investcorp is so entrepreneurial that there are lots of possibilities. If you invest in a blind pool fund, we might be able to offer you additional co-investment opportunities."

Second, we stand out because of our culture of collaboration. We have local teams with local pools of capital that collaborate globally. For example, our private equity team in India invests in India, but if they want to invest in an Indian company that is planning an IPO in the United States, we have the capability to make that happen.

Third, we welcome the kind of due diligence deep dive into environmental, social, and corporate governance regulations that is becoming standard. (I describe our ESG philosophy and practices in chapter 9.) "ESG used to be just one part of the normal due diligence, but now it's a standalone," Laura noted. "The standards keep rising and rising. The questions are getting deeper and more detailed, and they have more breadth. They're not just about the investment team. They're also getting into the DNA of the organization. That's a good thing, because we already subscribe to that."

ALL IN THE FAMILY

So where *did* our journey begin?

One promising starting point was family offices. Some of the largest have existed for a very long time, representing families like the Rockefellers in the United States, the Agnellis in Italy, the Rothschilds in the U.K., the Wallenbergs in Sweden, and the Quandts in Germany, who founded and still own BMW. But some of the wealthiest family offices were founded only in our lifetime: Walton Enterprises (from Walmart); Bezos Expeditions (from Amazon); Cascade Investment (from Microsoft); MSD Capital (from Dell Computer); Willett Advisors (from Bloomberg); KIRKBI (from LEGO toys); Pontegadea Inmobiliaria (from Inditex, the company that owns fast-fashion brands Zara and Massimo Dutti); and Blue Pool Capital (from Alibaba), to name just a few. There are literally thousands of these offices, representing an enormous amount of wealth, and the management of this wealth is increasingly becoming institutionalized.

"Thirty years ago, a private banker or investment placement specialist would meet directly with the individual who founded the business and created the wealth," recalled Yusef Al Yusef. "The decisions would be made based on relationships and emotions and trust. But that phenomenon has changed. The preservation of wealth has become a paramount focus—the 2008 global financial crisis is still reverberating—and the second and third generation are aware that making an investment decision is not straightforward. They are increasingly deciding, 'Let me hire an experienced specialist to take care of the due diligence of investment managers and asset allocation.' As a result, they have institutionalized the business by creating a family office, separating the investment business from the operating business."

Over the past two decades, the wealth controlled by family offices, especially in Asia and the Middle East, skyrocketed as many governments in these regions privatized what used to be public services, such as providing water and electricity. As a result, wealth shifted from the government to the family office of the company operating these services.

That's where we have a competitive edge. Not all family offices have the scale to be serviced by the Carlyles and Blackstones of the world. And even if they do, the market is so big and so fragmented that those targets may not be visible to those firms.

But they're visible to us. We've been servicing families in the Gulf for forty years. We know how they operate. And European, Asian, and U.S. family offices aren't all that different from Gulf family offices. Think of them as an obvious adjacent market that was practically inviting us to enter.

Family offices appreciate a one-stop solutions provider. "There aren't many firms that have the capability to offer private equity and real estate deals globally, along with credit management and investments in technology and infrastructure," Yusef pointed out. "We have a unique opportunity to be a global provider for family offices. That's a huge plus."

Another trend we could take advantage of: In many cases, the original funders of family offices are passing their wealth to the next generation. That generation often has different objectives and ideas about how they want to wield their wealth. For example, this is a generation that has matured with a close-up view of climate change; it has seen how disparities in healthcare can make the difference between life and death; it has watched the incredibly rapid evolution of technology and artificial intelligence. Many members of this generation want to put their money to "good" use. As Investcorp increasingly sharpens its focus on investing for sustainability (something I describe in chapter 9), we are especially well placed to offer advice.

But you don't want to put all your eggs in a family-office basket. "Family offices are the most fickle sort of institutional capital," Laura warned. "Many tend not to want to invest in blind pool funds. Marriages are typically perpetuated by pools of capital with decades of views of maintaining that capital. Most family offices haven't been around that long."

Whether long established or relatively new, family offices tend to tap into a shared network for investment advice. They talk with each other, exchange ideas, and suggest promising opportunities. It's an area where we stand out because of one intangible asset: our credibility.

THE CREDIBILITY QUOTIENT

Credibility is key to any successful investor relationship, but it's absolutely crucial with institutional investors. The community is tightly knit and there are no secrets. "Everyone talks to one another," Laura noted. "If Silver Lake is raising a new fund, every investor will call other investors: 'Why would you go into that fund?' If the initial commitment period for an existing fund is approaching its close, investors will ask each other: 'Will you re-up?' If someone decides to leave a fund, everyone wants to know why."

That's why brand and reputation are paramount. Because the relationship is long term, Laura continued, you cannot afford to abuse their hard-won trust. "You have to deliver on your promises about how you will invest their money. And if you deliver, they tend to stick with you for the next fund and the next fund and the next fund."

The good thing about the institutional community is that once you've established a relationship with a few institutions, you're known in the whole community. It's like moving into a new neighborhood: once you meet a few of the right neighbors and learn the language and culture, you fit in.

Building an institutional investor clientele is a slow and painstaking process. You do it one investor at a time. The competition is fierce, and you have to acknowledge that this is going to take a while. That's the point: to understand your growth so that you can seed the future.

I'm happy to say that our journey has already begun and we have a lot of momentum. In 2021, we partnered with two leading sovereign wealth funds from Southeast Asia in a new venture to acquire industrial real estate assets in the United States and leverage the growing demand for last-mile delivery logistics. More recently, we expanded our footprint in Southeast Asia with investment from Indonesia's sovereign wealth fund.

Our future won't be an either/or situation of either private clients or institutional investors, deal-by-deal transactions or blind pool funds. It will be powered by two engines that sit side by side. That will be a real game-changer for us.

When we say that we invest in partnership, we mean it. We're stewards of our clients' capital, whether they're individual investors or institutions. *Every* deal is important to us, and we're very careful about how we look after things. At the end of the day, that's Investcorp's key differentiator and ultimate added value.

CHAPTER 9

OPTIMIZING THE GROWTH ENGINES

In the previous chapters, I've talked about building the engines that enabled us to grow by scaling up existing businesses or acquiring or creating new businesses. In this chapter, I describe how we're servicing those growth engines to provide the best possible performance, both now and in the future, and both *for* now and *for* the future.

When I refer to our growth journey, I don't just mean a monetary goal of $50 billion in AUM or, since we surpassed that goal while this book was being written, our new goal of $100 billion in AUM. Of course, we want to achieve that goal and more. But the heart of those goals is making meaningful contributions every day to something much, *much* bigger.

What I'm talking about is sustainability.

Climate change presents the single biggest threat to our world as we know it. At the 2015 United Nations Climate Change Conference, held in Paris (also known as COP 21), 196 parties adopted a legally binding international treaty to promote sustainable development in order to reduce greenhouse gas emissions and limit global warming.

The topic of global sustainability may seem like a big stretch from the day-to-day details of running our business—or any of the businesses in our private equity portfolio—but in fact it's very relevant. As a global firm, we must constantly evaluate how our actions fit in a global context and adjust our strategy to address global issues. Sustainability is *the* most crucial issue facing the world today and tomorrow. Therefore, it must be a core part of our strategy.

So, what does this have to do with our growth engines? As we get bigger, we want them to perform in a way that supports and furthers global efforts to promote sustainability. How can we modify our growth engines to carry us forward along that path? The answer is by maintaining a sharp focus on our ESG agenda.

Short for Environmental, Social, and Governance, ESG is a way to consider the impact a company has on its employees, customers, and the communities in which it operates. Creating value for our shareholders may be our core raison d'être, but increasingly *value* has come to mean something more than financial returns. When we look at our balance sheet, we consider it in a much broader context: whether our business is a net positive for the world.

While ESG isn't a growth engine in itself, it is an important and increasingly necessary tool in servicing our growth engines and in refining them for optimal performance. Consequently, it's a part of everything we do.

TAKING OUR RESPONSIBILITIES SERIOUSLY

Investcorp has always been a socially responsible investor. The decision was made from the beginning to avoid investing in alcohol, tobacco, gambling, or defense equipment. (It was also decided not to invest in the petroleum industry, although in that case our reasoning was that because so much of the wealth of Gulf investors comes from oil, the firm already had plenty of indirect oil exposure.)

Similarly, we've always invested with a focus on long-term, sustainable growth. We have never been a firm that buys companies in order to break them up and sell off their assets. We have always sought to build our businesses and develop our real estate holdings to increase their value over the long term so that everyone benefits: shareholders, stakeholders, employees, and consumers.

But until a few years ago, even though the basic principles of ESG were seeded in our firm, we hadn't codified ESG as a comprehensive agenda. That's not surprising; over the past decade, even as investor interest in the overall topic exploded, different markets have focused on different aspects. Europe tended to zero in on environmental issues, particularly in identifying the risks associated with climate change and solutions to mitigate them through clean energy. The United States concentrated on how companies handled social issues, especially diversity, inclusion, and racial equality. Meanwhile, many emerging markets were ramping up their efforts to codify and strengthen their corporate governance, with a focus on anti-corruption measures, ethical procurement in the supply chain, better labor practices, and increased financial transparency.

In other words, previously we were investing sustainably as a matter of course. Now, we're consciously and deliberately investing *for* sustainability.

Here's a quick definition of terms: "Sustainable" investing draws from a broad spectrum of convictions, including faith-based investing, as well as the civil rights, antiwar, and environmental movements of the 1960s and 1970s. Nowadays, the terms "socially responsible investing" or "sustainable investing" are applied as a broad rubric covering a wide range of specific ESG-driven actions. The fundamental meaning is the same, however. It's how a company responds to the impact of a changing environment and a changing society to provide products and services in a way that has a quantifiably positive impact on the world.

The quantifiable element is crucial. Because the ESG lens is so nuanced, there's often a perception that the hype is much bigger than the substance. Avoiding that perception required us to create and apply a rigorous set of key performance indicators (KPIs) that can be measured and monitored on an ongoing basis. Only by following a disciplined approach can we demonstrate to our community of stakeholders—both internal and external, whether present or future employees or present or future clients—that we're genuinely committed to using the capital we've been entrusted with to create sustainable, long-term value.

That's where ESG comes in, not just as the tool that tweaks our growth engines but also as an auxiliary engine that provides an extra push in the right direction. Ironically, that push is not only about doing good but also about doing well.

To be blunt, the bigger we are and the more weight we can wield on the global stage, the more influence we can have in shaping a global sustainability agenda. So, it's a double win that investing with an ESG focus represents what Rishi Kapoor called "one of the most compelling secular investment opportunities for the next twenty to thirty years."

Consider the challenge of mitigating climate change. A critical mass of the global population has now accepted that this needs to be addressed, and that addressing it will require support from multiple stakeholders, significant amounts of capital, and investment on an unprecedented scale. Even addressing only the environmental aspects of climate change will require new technologies that will enable businesses and consumers to create and consume products and services in a way that is less carbon intensive.

To that end, Investcorp is presently evaluating five areas of focus for potential investment opportunities: power generation, such as solar, wind, and hydro; electrification of mobility, ranging from electric vehicles to aviation and shipping; storage of power; heavy industry, particularly carbon-intensive industries like agriculture and building construction; and carbon capture and sequestration. "These are areas that touch every aspect of our lives," Rishi said. "The good news is that two-thirds of those technologies have been invented. But it will require an investment of capital to scale up. That's where we can make a difference."

That's heady stuff. But there's more to sustainable investing than "just" environmental issues.

We have come to believe that *all* aspects of ESG are interconnected and inseparable, both for our portfolio companies and for our own organization. For us, the Social aspect of ESG extends beyond ensuring that our employees—and those of our portfolio companies—are treated fairly, and to investing in businesses that are seeking to give back to society in a sustainable manner. The Governance aspect means instilling a comprehensive system of checks and balances to guarantee that sustainability is baked into all our decisions and those of our portfolio companies.

When ESG initially took shape in the investment world's consciousness, there was a sense that it was an either/or proposition: either you did good or you did well. We have come to believe that operating a business with a focus on sustainability can *both* produce higher returns *and* address the most important issue defining our time: ensuring a sustainable future on our planet and among our communities.

That's even headier stuff.

Our ESG journey has evolved from introducing discrete "nice to have" initiatives to creating, coordinating, and implementing a "need to have" comprehensive business framework that aims to place ESG responsibility squarely at the core of the firm's culture, and that codifies and quantifies our behavior accordingly.

We take our responsibilities seriously. ESG concerns are top of mind for our present and prospective clients, as well as our present and future employees, so we want to get it right.

Starting in 2019, we committed—and have since renewed our priority and aim—to deliver value that is sustainable, inclusive, and considerate of all our stakeholders. This translates to how we operate as a global investment manager; how we interact with our employees and our portfolio companies; and how we connect with the world and the communities in which we operate. As part of that commitment, we have begun to share our thinking outside the firm. We want to forge a new path and inspire others to follow it.

This marks another significant step in the fundamental transformation of our company.

Our commitment is made concrete in our Responsible Business framework. The framework consists of three pillars of Investcorp's ESG responsibility: being a responsible citizen, being a responsible employer, and being a responsible operator. Each of the pillars is assigned KPIs to measure our behavior and that of our portfolio companies. We have a tangible implementable action plan within the firm's own operations and at the grassroots level for every company we invest in.

Let's examine how this plays out in practice.

PILLAR #1: BEING A RESPONSIBLE CITIZEN

This area of focus encompasses the myriad aspects of the "E" in ESG: energy management, water management, waste management, greenhouse gas emissions, and corporate social responsibility.

As described in chapter 7, we used India as our pilot for adopting and implementing an ESG framework throughout our portfolio companies by targeting investment opportunities in three key sectors: healthcare, financial services, and mass-market consumer products. Our strategy was to work with company founders from the "modern" generation, whose firms were already producing long-term value in a sustainable manner. We aimed to help them grow their business internationally, as well as within India.

One of our first investments was in NephroPlus, the leading dialysis service provider in India. Over the past two generations, the incidence of diabetes has increased dramatically, as middle- and upper-class Indians have exchanged a fiber-rich traditional diet for highly processed foods. In the early 1970s, roughly 3 percent of the urban population was diabetic. Two generations later, a 2017 study of fifteen states in India found that over 11 percent of Indian adults in large urban centers had diabetes.[1] As of 2019, 77 million adults were estimated to be affected by diabetes, putting India on track to surpass China as "the diabetes capital of the world."[2]

NephroPlus now has the largest network of dialysis centers in India, one that is over four times larger than the second-largest player in the industry, with more than 196 centers located in more than 115 cities. With a strong focus on patient-centric care, it is a strategic dialysis partner of choice for almost all the top hospitals in India. Since our investment, NephroPlus has not only continued to build its network of dialysis centers in India but has also expanded into select countries in Asia and the GCC, two other regions where diabetes is on the rise.

Their cost of treatment is a fraction of what you'd pay in Europe or the United States, and even the Middle East, for the same quality. The business has grown tremendously, as we expected, but it has grown by delivering good value to users, not just concerning dialysis treatment but also by making health and wellness accessible at an affordable price, when before it was not. As Rishi said, "It's about doing well and doing good at the same time."

FreshToHome is another classic ESG case study for us. As 2020 unfolded, we had been evaluating beneficiaries of the COVID-19 boost in e-commerce and health and hygiene awareness in India. One of the world's largest fully integrated online brands in fresh fish and meat, FreshToHome stood out for its creative use of state-of-the-art technology to provide a much more efficient mechanism for farmers and fishermen to deliver products directly to consumers in major cities across India. Thanks to a supply chain powered by artificial intelligence, FreshToHome was able to reduce food waste for suppliers to less than 2 percent—compared to 15 percent in traditional unorganized markets—while charging a fair price for products that are, as they promise, "100% Fresh and 0% Chemicals."

When we came across this business, we saw real opportunity for sustainable, long-term value creation. Having reliably fresh meat and seafood on a daily basis is hugely important in a market like India. We have thousands of customers who need and trust our products. We have hundreds of suppliers whose livelihoods have been significantly improved, because they can now sell their wares efficiently, with limited waste, at good prices. And we see a business that lends itself neatly to expansion into the Middle East; because the Middle East imports a lot of fresh meat and seafood from India, we could leverage Investcorp's understanding and reach in the region.

In November 2020, we participated in a $121 million funding round with other investors in FreshToHome. "The value Investcorp brings to the table is many times larger than the actual dollars and cents," Rishi noted. "By minimizing waste, we're clearly acting on the 'E' of ESG. By improving the livelihoods of thousands of fishermen in the coastal regions of India, we are delivering on the 'S.' By helping the company expand in a thoughtful, prudent manner, we're strengthening the 'G.' This is a win-win-win."

Our concern about the environment in which we all live, work, and connect with each other extends to the online world. One of our standout investments in this area is Impero, a U.K.-based market leader in safeguarding children online in a school environment. With computers in almost every classroom, children are exposed to influences ranging from the detrimental to the deadly, whether it's cyberbullying, political radicalization, or dangerous TikTok challenges.

Impero works with the police, children's advocacy groups, and nonprofit organizations in this space to identify the latest risk factors. Then its technology crunches and analyzes huge amounts of data. If a risk is flagged—for example, if there's an increase in online chatter about the so-called cotton ball diet, which is a dangerous and potentially deadly approach to weight loss, or a rise in research on suicide or mass shootings—then Impero will send an alert to the school and the school can intervene. It's a great example of using technology for social good.

Impero's software is now accessible in over eighty countries, including the United States and the U.K. The company has continued to grow both organically and through acquisitions, further expanding into new geographies, as it becomes increasingly important to address parents' and teachers' concerns about the online safety of children in the school environment.

We also focus on the physical places where we live, learn, and work. When Neil Hasson joined Investcorp in 2016 to head up our European real estate investment business, he recalled, "No one was asking about environmentally friendly building strategies. It wasn't that we weren't paying attention. It wasn't even on the radar screen. Now it's the first, second, and third question tenants and buyers ask."

There's no part of our organization that hasn't gone through a screening process for environmental responsibility. That includes our own operations. And that's why Investcorp initiated an environmental audit of our offices to determine what measures could be implemented over time to reduce our carbon footprint. As a result, our London office and U.S. data centers transitioned to 100 percent renewable energy sources.

Private equity firms like Investcorp can further leverage their environmental responsibility by ensuring that our portfolio of majority-owned investment assets across private equity and real estate, and even credit management, are all taking active steps to improve their carbon footprint. (I discuss this in more detail in the Conclusion.) Many of the businesses we invest in tend to be service-based industries, so they aren't heavily carbon intensive. Their carbon footprint manifests most in the power consumed in their buildings and the amount of travel their employees undertake, especially air travel. (By the way, Investcorp does not own a private jet. All our employees, including me, primarily fly commercial.) Nonetheless, we are focused on embedding a decarbonization framework while they're part of our portfolio, so they can continue on their own after they've left our fold.

At the same time, we're looking to invest in companies whose sole purpose is to help other firms reduce their carbon emissions. That way we come at the issue from both ends. And we've got a portfolio of assets that can use these technologies to help achieve those outcomes, so everyone benefits.

PILLAR #2: BEING A RESPONSIBLE EMPLOYER

This pillar of our Responsible Business framework covers the "S" part of ESG, from the health, safety, and well-being of employees to equitable pay and benefits, to diversity, equity, and inclusion (DE&I).

DE&I is one of the most high-profile issues in today's business world. Financial services, especially historically, had very little to do with DE&I—within the financial services, asset management especially; and within asset management, alternative asset management especially. There were very, *very* few alternative asset managers from diverse backgrounds, and that included not just gender but also education, ethnicity, and nationality.

That last part wasn't true at Investcorp, though. In addition to Nemir Kirdar, an Iraqi émigré, our three-co-founders were Mike Merritt, a former U.S. infantry officer in Vietnam; Elias Hallak, a financial wizard from Beirut; and Cem Cesmig, whose father was a Turkish Foreign Service officer. That original mix of nationalities remains to this day.

Other aspects of diversity were a challenge, however. Yusef Al Yusef, who heads up our private wealth platform in the Gulf, recalled that when he first joined Investcorp in the late 1990s, "the principals were men in Brioni suits who came from Chase Manhattan." Diversity, he joked, meant you came from Citibank.

However, as our business model became more global, we came to realize that diversity is what will best position us to overcome obstacles and create new, sustainable solutions. Research increasingly shows a close correlation between diversity and the likelihood of financial outperformance.[3] Furthermore, when your employees mirror the market—whether in terms of gender, ethnicity, or cultural background—they are better attuned to the unmet needs of consumers or clients like themselves. In short, a diverse workforce can be a potent source of innovation.[4]

More and more, we identify diversity as one of our core strengths. Having people who come to us with different ideas and who think differently from us opens our eyes to things we hadn't seen before. As Hazem Ben-Gacem likes to say, "Investing is all about judgment, and judgment comes from listening to a variety of views." But despite the growing body of evidence on how diverse teams boost bottom-line gains, progress on overall representation over the past five years was slower than we liked. That's why we are now taking a systematic approach to accelerate our DE&I practices across Investcorp.

It's often said that what gets measured shows what matters. To demonstrate our commitment to DE&I, we set specific targets that aim to elevate female professionals. The targets help ensure that we don't just have the right balance of women at all levels but also that we create the right environment, through professional development and work-life balance mechanisms, in which they can feel comfortable. Those targets are now assessed as part of our Internal Audit advisory review on ESG. (I describe the importance of the audit function in the next section.) "That spotlight on DE&I is extremely important because without it, managers might not naturally see the value," pointed out Habib Abdur-Rahman, who oversees Investcorp's sustainable investment strategy.

We recently launched a policy requiring that 50 percent of shortlisted job candidates come from diverse backgrounds. As a result, while managers are not forced to hire diverse talent, they *are* forced to consider it. "Oh, I can't find a qualified woman" is no longer a valid excuse.

We're making progress. Our pipeline is packed with diverse talent, and we're learning how to leverage it. Investcorp draws from a range broader than many firms twice its size. Our 500-some employees include people from forty-six different nationalities, of whom over one-third are now women; in 2021, nearly half (48 percent) of new hires were female, and among them, those for investment-focused roles increased to 51 percent in 2021. We've also launched mandatory training in unconscious bias. (I discuss our strategy in hiring and developing diverse talent in more detail in chapter 11.)

Furthermore, we're promoting our DE&I agenda in a larger arena. In 2021, Frances Townsend became the first woman to join Investcorp's Board of Directors. (Fran has been a member of our International Advisory Board since 2019.) Her appointment sent a signal throughout the firm. "I didn't know that my presence on the board would have any impact on Investcorp's diversity strategy," Fran recalled. "It was Jordana Semaan [who inaugurated the new position of Diversity & Inclusion Champion] who articulated to me what a boost it was to the whole program. She said, 'Every level of management understands that there's a different level of commitment and scrutiny just by your being there.'"

We're also trying to be a role model for the industry through our GP staking business. (The GP stands for General Partner, which refers to the management of the alternative asset company.) GP staking is a way to buy a non-control, minority interest in alternative asset firms. Anthony Maniscalco, who heads our GP staking business, explained: "Much the way Mubadala bought a minority interest in Investcorp, we buy 10 to 20 percent of their equity, which is used to fund the growth of their business by investing in their own funds and building out their teams. We can't control their decisions, but we can help them make better decisions."

One promising strategy is our partnership with Xponance, a $12 billion investment firm founded to seed interests in diverse and woman-owned alternative asset managers. "The universe of women- and minority-owned private equity firms has grown almost six times since 2014," noted Xponance's founder, Tina Byles Williams, adding that recent data show that diverse managers in the mid-market space have consistently outperformed the market, with the magnitude of outperformance also increasing over time.

Our partnership with Xponance acts as a "force multiplier" to expand opportunity for innovative investment strategies offered by diverse and women-owned firms. At the same time, there's a significant amount of capital flowing into diverse-owned GPs. "If you pick the right GPs that are diverse, those businesses should see more capital moving into their funds," said Anthony. "It's both a good investment and a positive thing to do."

We believe that our approach will help accelerate this trend by increasing access to the type of strategic capital and other resources needed to help these firms further expand and strengthen their businesses.

The benefits of partnering with Xponance go both ways. "Tina and her partners have helped our partners that aren't diverse owned to think through diversity in a practical sense, to have a better understanding of what it means to hire and build a diverse workforce," Anthony said.

PILLAR #3: BEING A RESPONSIBLE OPERATOR

While Governance—the "G" in ESG, and the third pillar in our Responsible Business framework—may not be as "sexy" as environmental and social issues in the ESG triumvirate, it's the fundamental platform that everything rests on: business ethics, a strong and fair system of checks and balances in how Investcorp and our portfolio companies are run, transparency in our policies, privacy protections, and quality and safety controls. Being a responsible operator is crucial to building trust and confidence among all Investcorp's stakeholders.

Good governance has been core to Investcorp from its inception. The vast majority of private equity firms were—and are—initially set up as partnerships, with two or three senior partners in charge, and they are run along partnership lines—a business version of "our club, our rules." Unfortunately, too often this can lead to situations where shareholders want to get into the pilot's seat and try to fly the plane. Investcorp was set up as a corporate entity. From the very beginning, we voluntarily agreed to a lot of regulatory oversight, with clear separation between ownership and management, and a board that ensured the cockpit door stayed locked.

Governance is what has kept us on the right track during our growth journey. "It provides assurance to the senior management and board of directors that the internal controls—the key processes and the people who control those processes and make the decisions—are operating as designed and mitigating the risks within the organization," explained Fortune Chigwende, who heads our Internal Audit operations.

Our governance framework is built with three "lines of defense." The first line of defense self-checks and reports on how each line of business (LOB) is managed: its strategy, how that strategy is executed, the checks and balances, the reporting structures, and the frequency of those reports. Basically, it's about what makes you successful as a business. The second line of defense is essentially another pair of eyes analyzing and double-checking each LOB's risk management and compliance processes to make sure we're following the proper guidelines and regulations. The third line of defense is the Internal Audit function. "We come in independently to certify to the Executive Chairman, the Executive Committee, and the Board of Directors whether all those controls are good enough, aligned to our risk appetite and operating effectively," Fortune said.

As part of our transformation, we needed to build our muscles to lift heavier weights and to train those muscles to do different things. The Internal Audit function is like a training coach. It has a unique ability to look across the business and identify areas where things aren't done consistently. It interacts with all the teams in all our locations around the world, then provides insights on all aspects of their operations, such as on ESG implementation by each line of business and in each geography.

Our governance framework extends to our portfolio companies. In our business, we take risks every day, and a lot of the value that we derive from our businesses results because we've put the right governance structures in place at the beginning. Every company we invest in has to have an audit committee, and Investcorp representatives have to be part of it. The checks and balances comprise everything from standard bylaws, such as precluding the CEO from borrowing $1 million from the company's coffers, to cybersecurity, to strategies for succession planning.

We build a board of directors with appropriate expertise, who can really add value, not just tick off boxes. We put in place proper incentives for management. We don't want to step into management's shoes (or onto their toes), but our job is to help family-owned businesses transition to professional organizations—organizations that may eventually become public companies. As such, we have a responsibility to instill and enforce good governance.

Savio Tung, one of our senior advisors, noted that among the more than 100 companies whose acquisitions he oversaw, he replaced nearly half their CEOs. "That's exercising governance. We're here to help mitigate the risk for our shareholders and achieve good investment returns. If the CEOs don't perform, I have to take action." (For example, it's unlikely that the House of Gucci would have survived if Maurizio Gucci had continued as CEO, let alone transform from a troubled money pit into one of Wall Street's hot stocks.)

Part of being a responsible operator is embedding sustainability considerations in every part of the business, from Investcorp itself to the newest addition in our investment portfolio. As proof of our commitment, in 2021 Investcorp became a signatory to the United Nations Principles for Responsible Investment (UN PRI). The UN PRI is a global standard that seeks to codify a language of good practices built on sustainability. That's important because initiatives flourish when people have a common understanding of what to achieve and how to achieve it.

Our investors were increasingly asking us when—not whether—we were going to sign on to the UN PRI, but taking action was not a simple matter of scrawling an attestation on an official form. "The PRI is a very detailed set of standards and recommendations of what constitute best practices," explained Habib Abdur-Rahman. "The UN PRI asks you questions and scores you accordingly. For example, it asks whether climate change is included in your investment decisions, recommends fifteen ways to integrate climate change into your strategy, and then scores you on how you implement those recommendations."

If you're a signatory to the UN PRI, it's a signal of your long-term intentions concerning ESG. It requires a lot of resources to do it right: people, time, and capital. It's not like you can just pick it up. You can try to game the PRI, but the organization increasingly audits what is submitted. So, the PRI is a proxy for good practices within an organization concerning ESG and sustainability. We're proud to do our part.

INVESTING IN TOMORROW

In just a short time, ESG has become a core requirement for more and more of our shareholders and stakeholders around the world—not just present and prospective investors but also among the talent pool of present and prospective employees. A recent McKinsey study found that 82 percent of survey participants in U.S. companies listed "contributing to society" and "creating meaningful work" as their top two priorities.[5] If you don't have ESG credentials, those potential employees won't even think about you. That's why ESG is not something we merely tip our hat to. It has become a conscious consideration in our decision-making.

How ESG will work in the future is something we need to figure out for the good of the organization, our portfolio companies, and the world we all live in. As an organization with investors, employees, customers, and suppliers spread around the globe, we want to be a responsible global citizen.

We're working to improve the lives of future generations. Tomorrow should be an improvement over today.

CHAPTER 10

"LIKE FALLING OFF A CLIFF"

I n mid-January 2020, I and a few members of the Operating Committee spent a week traveling around Asia, on a road show to meet present and potential investors. After two days in Singapore, we arrived in Beijing, where for three days we met with senior finance and government officials. There were some rumors of "this virus thing in Wuhan," co-CEO Hazem Ben-Gacem recalled, but no one seemed concerned. "We thought, *Oh, it's another bird flu. It's like SARS. It won't affect us much.*"

We visited Tiananmen Square, shivering in the frigid January wind. To warm up, Hazem and I went into the three-story Kentucky Fried Chicken outlet there, famous for being the first KFC in China and, when it opened in 1987, the largest in the world. "That's how oblivious we were," Hazem said later. "No one wore masks. No one imagined a world-wide pandemic."

From Beijing, I continued to Tokyo, then New York and London; I hosted an off-site meeting of the Operating Committee at the end of the month, and finally flew back to the Gulf in March—a typical round-the-world itinerary for the leader of a global investment firm.

It would be the last trip I would take for over fourteen months.

At the OpCom meeting, International Advisory Board member Mohamed El-Erian dialed in. The former chairman of U.S. President Obama's Global Development Council and frequent commentator for Bloomberg, CNBC, and the *Financial Times*, Mohamed generally modifies his language in public but doesn't mince words in private. He sounded the alarm about what was now called COVID-19, describing what pandemics do to economies, people, and human interactions. He said, "Normally, an economy starts slowing down and people spend less on things. It's a gradual change. But this is different. This will be a sudden stop. It will be like falling off a cliff."

We heard what he was saying, but we didn't have a full understanding of what it actually meant in practice. We soon found out.

The beauty of leading a business with offices stretching from Beijing to New York is that you get to take the pulse of the world on a daily basis. It was clear where we were heading.

By the time I returned to Oman, cases of COVID-19 were multiplying around the world. Colleagues were being met at airports by personnel in hazmat suits. Borders were closing. Major cities were imposing quarantines, then lockdowns. I wasn't allowed to hug my family—my wife, my kids, or my grandkids. I realized this would be serious.

Then the news came of the first Investcorp employee to be stricken with the disease, a twenty-seven-year-old man working in the New York office. When I called him, he told me he had just been released from intensive care. The way he was coughing and struggling to breathe while trying to talk—it was really scary.

I asked, "What medicine are they giving you?"

He gasped, "They're giving me everything."

Normally, if someone has cancer, there's a treatment protocol. If someone has diabetes, they're given insulin. If you break your arm, they set the bone and put you in a cast. But here was a young guy being hammered so badly, and no one seemed to know what to do. What was especially distressing was that he had to be isolated in an apartment, forced to stay away from his family, trying to recover on his own. Someone would bring food and leave it outside the door.

I thought, *Not only do we not know what this does to human beings, but we don't know how to treat it.* I'd never felt such helplessness.

A LUCKY BREAK

Who could have guessed that antiquated technology would sow the seeds of Investcorp's salvation?

Like many companies around the world, COVID caught us by surprise. Unlike most companies, though, we were able to immediately and seamlessly shift to remote work—owing entirely to an embarrassing public technical glitch five years earlier.

Before 2015, Investcorp hadn't prioritized spending money on technology, investing only the bare minimum to keep things running. By 2015, the client reporting system in the Gulf, which had been custom-built back in the 1980s, was limping along on its last legs. Dedicated inter-office telephone lines often went down, which stymied data sharing. There was a decades-long backlog of upgrades demanding to be addressed. "We were on version 5 of some software, while the industry was on version 17," said then Chief Administrative Officer Ramzi AbdelJaber. "Some versions were so old that Microsoft no longer supported them."

My first town hall meeting was my introduction to the entire company, and the tech support team was determined that everything would run seamlessly. To ensure that the overhead cameras wouldn't accidentally come loose from their mounts, Najib Rahal, now our Chief Information Officer, personally duct-taped all the cameras to the ceiling, then painted the duct tape to blend in with the ceiling. The rehearsal was flawless.

Then came the actual town hall.

I cued up my PowerPoint presentation—and on the third slide, the PowerPoint minimized and froze. The tech team rebooted my laptop, but it didn't work. They did it again with the same non-result. I wasn't able to show anything on the screen. Najib had to manually oversize each slide so I could proceed with the presentation.

It later turned out that the problem was a faulty clicker: the button to advance to the next slide had jammed. And with one click—or rather, the lack of one click—our need to upgrade our technology became front and center.

The glitch galvanized a digitization agenda that leapfrogged us from outdated technology straight into cutting-edge cloud computing. "When I joined the firm in 2014, part of my role was to help us get the operations up to par. I recommended that we not look five years ahead but to the future of technology: distributed services, remote access, the cloud. At the time, working in the cloud was revolutionary—certainly for Investcorp, but also for the industry," Najib said.

The gamble paid off. That same year, we deployed a virtualization layer. Now, instead of having clunky desktop computers, all someone needed was a monitor and a connection to our system. This was clearly the direction to take. We were becoming more global, which meant that our people would be traveling more. They needed to access information that would enable them to be "in the office" even when they were physically elsewhere. For an international firm to implement this at scale was cutting edge in the industry at the time.

Over the next few years, Investcorp employees became used to working remotely. But did we think all our work could effectively be done from home? Of course not. No one had ever done it before.

In early March 2020, as COVID was overwhelming country after country, we assembled a global task force to monitor the situation in local regions. But it was clear that handing out bottles of hand sanitizer and posting signs reminding people to wash their hands was futile. By the beginning of the second week of March, employees were allowed to choose to work remotely. At that point, Ramzi asked Najib for an action plan. Najib replied, "Just tell everyone to go home and turn on their device. You don't need to do anything differently."

On March 12, 2020—a Thursday—we announced that we were closing our offices for the next two weeks. Our 400-some employees were seamlessly working from home by the weekend. "Other firms were scrambling for laptops and monitors," Ramzi said. "But because of the technological architecture we had, you could log in from any device—a PC, a Mac, an iPad, even your phone. If you had anything at home, you could log in. That was massive." Najib agreed, "Everything was business as usual."

Except, of course, it wasn't.

"THIS IS NOT THE RIGHT TIME
TO GET RID OF ANYONE"

At the first meeting of the Operating Committee under lockdown, for the first time in this business, making money or making a profit wasn't a priority on my agenda. Infection numbers were climbing, and people were terrified to even go outside. My top concern was for our people to stay safe and be able to look after their families.

Just about every OpCom member assumed we would lay off staff or, at least, follow the lead of other financial firms and furlough people. We couldn't deny that many things were going the wrong way. Some of our portfolio companies were collapsing. Our earnings were being impacted. But, as Daniel Lopez-Cruz, then the head of our European private equity team, recalled, "Mohammed was very clear that he didn't want to consider staff reductions. He said, 'We're not even discussing it. This is not the right time to get rid of anyone.'" (A quick note here: I include more contributions than usual from team members in this chapter because COVID affected us all and surviving COVID took the efforts of our entire organization.)

My rationale was simple. I knew we were a strong company. Our balance sheet was in good shape. We could afford to look after our people—and we had to: they were our core asset. We needed to keep the teams intact, because that's how we could come back when the situation stabilized. When they needed help and reassurance, they needed to know that Investcorp would be with them.

As a result, we didn't have any job cuts. Even though there were some individuals who were due to be terminated because of poor performance, this was not the right time to say goodbye to anyone. In fact, we reduced senior people's compensation in order to protect junior people's jobs.

I repeated that message in frequent calls with the Executive Committee. Hazem recalled, "[Co-CEO] Rishi [Kapoor] and I would want to talk about the business. Mohammed would interrupt to ask about our people—one of our guys was stuck in Bahrain while his children were quarantined in Mumbai, another had both parents in hospital with COVID. Mohammed is a military man and doesn't wear his emotions on his sleeve, but now I saw a very different man. He had so much compassion. And that set the right tone for Rishi, myself, and the senior leadership."

We tried to maintain that tone in the bi-weekly virtual town hall meetings I held with our co-CEOs. Town halls pre-COVID typically involved the business heads describing their view of the business and laying out the next steps. The town halls during COVID were different.

Richard Kramer, the then head of Risk Management and now our Chief Operating Officer, recalled, "People from different offices at any level were invited to come online and share their life from a COVID perspective: What was it like to be cooped up in your apartment in New York compared with your colleagues in Singapore or London? What rituals did you and your family have that kept you going? I loved that. It was an insight into colleagues that we hadn't had before. It was both cathartic and very humanizing."

To be honest, there was no question in my mind that this just seemed to be the right thing to do. When we look back, how will firms be judged during this period—by their income, by a particular IPO, or a company sale? These are important, but there are some things that are more important. In my opinion, leading an organization involves more than numbers in an annual report. And I hope every one of our people will have some stories of how Investcorp helped them during this extraordinary time.

PROPPING UP THE PORTFOLIO

While we were working from home, our portfolio companies were on the front lines. The big concern was: Are they running out of cash? We owned some supply chain and food production and distribution businesses that never shut because they were deemed essential. But with some of our other companies, their revenue simply collapsed.

Our number one priority was protect the people. In the beginning, no one knew what that meant. COVID hit so quickly that we and our companies were flung into a maelstrom, with no chance to prepare ourselves. What served as our compass and stabilizer was an intense focus on cash. That was priority number two: make sure our businesses had enough cash to keep going.

Unlike some private equity firms, we try not to overload our businesses with debt. We have some debt, of course, but we never push it to the limit. That was beneficial now. We tapped into Investcorp's balance sheet and drew on our credit lines to make sure we had liquidity for the firm. We had our portfolio companies draw down *their* credit lines. In addition, we put our companies through a stringent screening process to identify ways they could save money or simply not spend it. The objective was to build a robust fortress for the firm and for our investments, and the first step was to ensure sufficient liquidity.

Our private equity teams implemented an intense new protocol: weekly team calls to tightly monitor cash flow, combined with very short-term cash-flow forecasting to try to look around the corner into the next week, next month, and next quarter. Then, they built speculative scenarios for each time period. (We also built a "shadow book" for Investcorp itself, a stress test that evaluated how COVID might affect the value of its investments. It was an effective road map showing where the profitability of the firm might go and, I'm glad to say, proved remarkably accurate.)

In late March 2020, Daniel Lopez-Cruz and Dave Tayeh—the

respective heads of our European and North American Private Equity portfolios—were asked to get in front of our investors and provide our views. "Our investors were panicking a little and we didn't have any materials prepared to reassure them," Daniel recalled. "What I told them was, 'We'll take a hit and some companies will lose cash, but I am reasonably comfortable that we will salvage the whole portfolio.' What I thought was, *I hope I don't have to swallow my words.* But, in fact, it happened the way we predicted."

We doubled down on our support. "The whole team was in lockdown, no one was traveling, so everyone was focusing exclusively on the portfolio," Daniel said. "We will never have that amount of brain power focused on those companies again."

In the end, among the eleven companies Daniel oversaw in the European Private Equity portfolio, only two or three had real issues. The worst affected was Vivaticket, a global provider of ticketing software to the leisure and entertainment industries, sports, cultural events, and trade shows in more than fifty countries, which we had bought just the previous September. If you wanted to visit Walt Disney World, catch an exhibition at the Musée du Louvre, attend a concert, or snag a seat at an FC Barcelona game, the transaction went through Vivaticket. Now, that had all evaporated: on one day in March 2020, Vivaticket's CEO reported, they sold just twelve tickets. Over the next year, between closures, postponed tours, or canceled shows, the company sold exactly half the tickets they had in 2019.

Fortunately, a significant section of Vivaticket's business was contractual, so it had long-term revenue—not much but enough, with stringent budgeting, to keep it afloat. And every time a window of trust opened—whether it was limiting the number of visitors, staggered time slots at museums, rules about masking in theaters and sports stadiums, or even the roll-out of vaccines—people were desperate to get out of the house and buy an experience. Millions of tickets were sold.

What really kept us afloat and on course was that Investcorp had learned some hard lessons during the 2008 financial cataclysm. These lessons now shielded us from the worst effects of the pandemic. Few of our companies were in cyclical businesses, and almost none was directly consumer facing. The firm was much better defended than it had been twelve years earlier.

We had no capital-intensive businesses, no manufacturing businesses, no hotels. You can make a lot of money from those businesses, but you've got high fixed-operating costs, which can make you vulnerable. We had shifted to business services and businesses that were reliant on the talent of people rather than on manufacturing capabilities. In real estate, 95 percent of our portfolio was in warehousing and multi-family rentals. We had focused on warehousing, because regardless of what happens in the retail world, you still need distribution centers, whether you're distributing to physical shops or via online retail channels. You win both ways. Likewise, people have to have somewhere to live and that involves a long-term lease, whereas with hotels, the length of a lease is one night. Now that paid off, especially as online shopping skyrocketed.

We were able to do business, and that's something we were not able to do in 2008–2009. During that earlier period, business stopped; we did no new transactions at all. We didn't have those issues this time, though. We kept looking for areas to invest in. And we found them.

For example, in February 2020, Investcorp acquired Fortune Fish & Gourmet, one of the largest distributors of fresh and frozen seafood and specialty foods in the United States. While Fortune's restaurant clients took a hit—"75% of our customers shut down at the onset of COVID-19," reported Fortune CEO Sean O'Scannlain—its retail business exploded, as it signed on with Whole Foods and began creating products for at-home meal kits. Fortune actually grew during the pandemic and set a record year in 2021.

We closed on a lot of add-on acquisitions for the portfolio that were both set up and stitched down during the height of COVID. Nine months after we acquired Fortune, we helped them acquire Neesvig's, a

Wisconsin-based purveyor of top-quality meats, poultry, and seafood. It was Fortune's largest transaction yet, and it further expanded its brand.

Between March 2020 and March 2021, Dave Tayeh's team closed on half a dozen acquisitions across the portfolio—twice as many as before the pandemic. "The real drivers were that we were super-connected to our portfolio companies, we didn't have too much debt so we had flexibility, and we were investing in sectors in which, even if they were impacted by COVID, the impact was relatively short-lived, so once we felt better about future prospects, we could be aggressive," he explained.

COVID also made the seller base more receptive. The owner of Neesvig's had owned the business for over thirty years and was in his late sixties. "Something like COVID happened and he was ready to get out and slow down," Dave said. "If you were the right guy, he was ready to have the conversation."

We were "the right guy" a lot. We never stopped *doing* business. All in all, we were more productive during that time than we had been pre-COVID. And the wonderful thing is, we did not lose a single company across our portfolio. Some of that was because we were in the right industries, in the right spaces. Much was due to the way our teams reacted. Chalk it up to judgment or luck—either way, we came out far better than we could have expected. By the end of 2020, Investcorp posted a record AUM of $32.2 billion.

The message was this: We're strong enough to survive this and strong enough not to sit on the sidelines. If there are opportunities, we're strong enough to take them.

THE HUMAN FACTOR

Just because life under COVID became the new normal, that didn't mean we *felt* normal. We had initially announced in mid-March 2020 that our offices would close for two weeks. That turned into "We will be operating remotely until the end of the month." The return date was then postponed to June, then to the beginning of September. "We didn't open the New York office for anything except voluntary occupancy for eighteen months," recalled Pete Rommeney, our head of Human Resources.

The firm's technology worked well. The problem was that most people weren't set up for working at home. Before COVID, it was fine to flip open your laptop at the kitchen table for a few hours after your kids went to bed, knock out some emails, and maybe polish a report. Now, people were working from home for ten hours a day and were expected to produce the same quantity and quality of work as they had done when they were in the office. At the beginning, it was impossible to find a comfortable desk chair or buy printer ink. People were jockeying with their spouses and kids for internet access and battery chargers. "We heard about people putting up cardboard partitions on the kitchen table, so everyone could have their designated space," Pete said. "And if you were living in New York City, you constantly heard ambulances going up and down the street," which was both disturbing and distracting.

There was a clear recognition that the pandemic was impacting our people's mental and physical health. At one of our town halls, I said, "Listen, we all have our difficult moments. It's okay to not always be okay." This is a business in which people are used to setting—and achieving—stratospheric expectations for themselves. We knew nobody was trying to take advantage of the situation to take an extra nap; but they needed permission to acknowledge their human frailty.

We were already providing full-on technical support so they could keep working. It seemed only right that we should provide emotional support, too. When employees reported getting frazzled from twelve hours of back-to-back video calls or the stresses of working at home, we offered everyone a free subscription to the Headspace meditation app. We also made free counseling available for any topic, whether it was related to work or to personal issues.

Pete Rommeney and his team spent a lot of time, especially in the early days, checking in with people to make sure they had everything they needed to do their work well. "We weren't just addressing the concerns of people reaching out to us. We proactively reached out to them. Human Resources had a global list of all our employees, and we'd go down the list, name by name, and someone would personally call each employee every two weeks. You can do that with a 500-person firm. I had about 100 names on my list, then we'd switch so that I'd take someone else's list and they'd take mine. If anyone was struggling—their father had been hospitalized or there was a lot of friction in their household—we'd contact their head of business and have *them* check in."

We created a new one-year appointment of an "office lead"—one for the United States, one in Europe, and one in Bahrain—whose responsibility was to tend to morale. We deliberately chose senior leaders, rather than the heads of the LOBs, because they were closer to the employee base.

Mike O'Brien in our U.S. real estate group was appointed to look after things in the United States. "Mohammed was concerned that with so many people working remotely, they would lose touch with the culture of the firm. Our culture was what would help us recover and grow, so it was extremely important to preserve it," Mike recalled. "He told me, 'We're going to get out of this through leadership. You're going to set an example of how to do business.'"

Mike initially tried to discuss with me how the business was doing, but, he remembered, "Mohammed didn't want to hear it. He wanted to know how people were doing, what was the vibe in the office and in the industry, what we could do to encourage people to return to the office when the time would be right [to do so]. We didn't want to be the first company to ask people to come back but we didn't want to be the last, either."

The office leads would be an important input that, eventually, contributed to the decision as to when and how to reopen our offices. Meanwhile, we also urged our team leaders to reach out to their team members and come up with their own ways to stay connected. Like many of our teams, Dave Tayeh's team implemented a voluntary weekly happy hour.

A different person each week was assigned to create a game—a virtual treasure hunt or a trivia contest, or Investcorp's version of *Hollywood Squares*—then everyone would raise a glass. "In a weird way, it was better for the team," Dave said. Pre-COVID, team members traveled so much that there was no opportunity for socializing. The online get-togethers fostered greater cohesion among all the team members, up and down the ranks.

"We were given guidance, and we also figured out our own ideas to support our teams," recalled Anthony Maniscalco, who heads our GP staking business. He frequently reminded his people that we'd been through challenges in the past, and we could get through this one, too. Some of his team members had very young children; "you'd hear babies screaming in the background and you'd just feel for them."

One associate had a newborn and a spouse who was experiencing a lot of personal pressures and suffering anxiety. As a father of four whose first children were twins born just after he relocated to London, Anthony could sympathize. "We gave him a lot of rope to deal with that situation, rather than pressure him on the work side. My wife talked with his wife and was able to offer some comfort. We just wanted him to do what was best for his wife, his baby, and his family," Anthony said. "COVID reminded us that life is fragile, and you've got to take care of your own, whether it's your family or your team."

On a much bigger scale, Investcorp and our partners pitched in to aid global efforts in combatting the disease. In Bahrain, we sponsored free meals, donated masks and medical gowns, and contributed $1 million to Bahrain's Royal Humanitarian Foundation. In the United States, AlixPartners provided pro bono advice to help manufacturing companies retool to produce critical medical supplies.

Our portfolio companies stepped up, too. Fortune International partnered with a Chicago-based food pantry to donate food and supplies to families impacted by COVID-19. In Europe, Dainese, a company that makes gear and sportswear for motorcycling enthusiasts, pivoted to producing protective clothing for medical staff. Eviivo, a software provider for small and medium-sized accommodations businesses, partnered with its customers to make available 15,000 hotel rooms across the U.K. for National Health Service workers. In Abu Dhabi, Reem Integrated Healthcare Holdings built an eighty-bed hospital in fifteen days in response to the pandemic. And in India, Bewakoof, an online shopping site, revamped its manufacturing lines to produce masks, sanitizers, and personal protective equipment kits.

In May 2020, we ran a company-wide employee engagement survey. The entire firm had been working remotely for three months by then. One of the highest-scoring items was "faith in leadership." That spoke to our communications strategy, whether it was company-wide town halls or individual leaders looking after the welfare of their team members. In addition, people had high confidence in the firm and enjoyed working at Investcorp. That was very heartening.

REEXAMINING OUR PRIORITIES

The pandemic accelerated a number of changes for Investcorp, while etching lasting results in the firm's procedures, work patterns, and culture.

The use of remote technology is now second nature, which has both plusses and minuses. You would think it would make it more difficult to build and foster the kind of deep relationships with our clients that Investcorp is known for, but paradoxically, remote technology has enabled us to connect more closely with them. With established clients, we found that when people have been dealing with your firm for forty years, they don't need to see you in person.

Similarly, by moving from physical road shows to virtual ones, I became actually more available to existing and potential clients. Normally, on road shows, you block out a couple of weeks to visit different regions. The schedule is fixed, the flights booked, meetings and dinners are marked on the calendar. If someone happens to be out of town during your visit, you can't see them. With videoconferencing, though, I can host a teleconference in Kuwait in the morning, followed by another in London after lunch, and conclude with a late afternoon e-meeting in New York, all without leaving my desk. This gives us an additional tool we didn't think we had.

We're not just more efficient but also more productive. By our not sitting in airports, sitting in taxis, and sitting in airplanes, the number of client interactions between 2020 and 2021 increased 35 percent over the previous year. And it's better for our carbon footprint.

Yet that efficiency came at a price. The same engagement survey found that working remotely did not improve work-life balance. In fact, it had the opposite effect. The technology has gotten so good that you're never unplugged. "I would be online 12 hours a day," Richard Kramer noted. "I've never worked so hard." After month upon month at this pace, some really talented people walked away. They were just burned out.

For others, especially new hires, the distance makes it difficult to deepen employee engagement. We have people whom we recruited virtually, interviewed virtually, onboarded virtually, and manage virtually. Until recently, they hadn't seen the front door of an Investcorp office in their career.

"We can't lose the personal contact—the teaching, the mentorship, the apprenticeship of younger people," Anthony Maniscalco said. "We have to continue to do that. But if someone needs to work from home on a Friday, so long as they are working, that's absolutely fine. If I have a 7:30 a.m. call, I no longer have to catch a 6 a.m. train to commute to the office. I can wake up at 6, exercise, and then do the call. We just have to have a process to ensure people don't fall through the cracks if they work from home."

COVID caused everyone to reexamine their lives and their priorities. As we began to emerge from the tunnel, some people couldn't wait to get back to the office. Others had second thoughts. One senior person told Pete Rommeney, "For the first time in twenty years, I've been having dinner with my family. I'm not giving that up anymore."

Further, COVID caused us to reexamine our priorities as a firm. To be sure, we're still focused on making a profit. But we also want to ensure that our people feel safe and supported. Finding a sustainable harmony of remote work and work-life balance is something we know we'll have to address, both to attract new talent and to retain existing employees. For now, it's an ongoing experiment.

Certainly, there were big question marks in the spring and summer of 2020. When Investcorp's fiscal year ended on June 30, 2020, we posted a loss for only the second time in our history. But the combination of renewed confidence and a corporate culture now marked by compassion was a winner. We blew through what we thought we could do. Fiscal years 2021 and 2022 were not only profitable but also exceeded our AUM targets. By our fortieth anniversary in 2022, Investcorp had posted over $40 billion in AUM.

After two years of turmoil, we were ready to turn the page to begin a new chapter.

CHAPTER 11

FUTURE-PROOFING THE FIRM

I n 2022, Investcorp celebrated its fortieth anniversary. The question on everyone's mind was: How can we ensure that we'll be around for another forty years?

Our business is all about measuring and managing risk. Many people assume that "risk" means external risks: a pandemic, a recession, or a geopolitical crisis. Certainly, we've seen all three over the past three years. All of them burst upon us with little or no warning.

You can't predict when life will throw you a curve ball. What you *can* do is prepare for how you will respond—because the only certainty is that external factors magnify and amplify internal issues. That means identifying and remediating internal risks. As part of our ongoing transformation, we are focusing on five key areas where Investcorp is reinventing and reinforcing itself to confront the challenges ahead.

CHALLENGE: ATTRACTING, DEVELOPING, AND RETAINING THE RIGHT TALENT

During a break at an OpCom meeting in 2019, some of the members were chatting about how old they were. As one after another shared their birthdates, they realized that eight out of the fourteen members were all roughly the same age: fifty-seven years old. It was not a pleasant discovery.

"A concentration around a certain age means less diversity among generations. Older, experienced heads need younger ideas," commented Tim Mattar. "Furthermore, we realized, 'Oh, boy, a number of people will soon be thinking about the next steps in their career. We can't have half of OpCom retiring at the same time.'"

It was a call to sharpen our focus on talent development: becoming a magnet for top talent, identifying the people who could lead the business going forward, and training managers to nurture them.

People are the biggest risk in our business. Despite all the talk about algorithms and quantitative analysis, investment management is, at heart, a judgment business; and judgment depends on people. They are not just our most important asset, they are our *only* asset. Losing people in key positions is a risk. Putting people into positions where they don't work out is a risk. Hiring the wrong people is a risk.

One way we have tried to mitigate the risks concerning people is by growing our own talent. Most of the senior people at Investcorp today grew up in the firm and are steeped in its culture. They exemplify our principles and demonstrate the possibilities associated with a career here. But we've also seen—and not too long ago—how insularity can be a risk. It can lead to bias, to blind spots, to a "not-invented-here" syndrome of settling into habitual ways of seeing things and doing things—and of dismissing ideas from outside.

That's why we need a combination of people from a variety of backgrounds. If our homegrown talent serves as the firm's spine, new people are the muscles that give us the strength and flexibility to try new things. We need new blood to challenge ourselves and bring in different perspectives.

Because this is a people business, we have to attract world-class talent or else it will be impossible to become world-class investors. I will say, though, that while we always want to upgrade our talent, we want to do it the right way. Stars and "rainmakers" aren't part of our culture. We can't afford the risk that they will arouse envy and demotivate their colleagues.

How can we become a talent magnet? In this industry, top performers and high-potential talent are typically driven by financial compensation and accelerated career progression. I'm not going to discuss the former here, but I can certainly attest to the latter. Fortunately, this is one area in which Investcorp stands out because of how we approach career development. (I talk more about our culture in the next section.)

Really smart people don't just demand intellectual engagement; they *need* the opportunity to learn and add value to themselves as individuals. They want to do things they haven't done before, preferably in a collaborative and respectful culture. There's a bonus if they can help build something that's bigger than themselves. That's a common denominator, whether they're recent university graduates or people with years of experience.

We're looking for junior people who want to explore a world of possibilities. And we're looking for senior people like Jan Erik Back and Pete Rommeney, both of whom were content *enough* at their previous companies but were getting a bit bored. "To see a firm that really wanted to go somewhere and to be part of that journey was something that really attracted me," was how Jan Erik put it. "Investcorp presented a firm with global aspirations that combined a forty-year track record of success with an entrepreneurial mindset," said Pete. "It was a unique opportunity that I couldn't find anywhere else."

That's the message we want to put out there: This isn't a place to be content. It's a place where you can grow and be part of something special.

What further differentiates us in the global talent competition is the opportunity to have a truly global perspective. We literally operate around the world. A statistic we're all proud of is that our nearly 500 employees come from fifty different countries of origin. Over one-third are women.

We aim to mirror our present markets and reflect future ones. The future is diverse, and both employees and investors want to be part of something they can relate to. Jordana Semaan, our DE&I champion, likes to say that unless you have all twenty-six letters of the alphabet, you can't string together full sentences; if you're missing letters, people won't understand you. We want the full complement of talent, from A to Z.

Because the markets with the greatest growth potential have predominantly young populations, we're pushing to hire younger people. At the same time, however, we know that Gen Z and Millennials have been the cohort driving the post-COVID "Great Resignation."[1]

How, then, can we persuade them—and all our top talent—to stay?

One of my major preoccupations is removing the roadblocks from our teams to ensure that people continue to grow. We don't generally send people on supplemental courses or subsidize MBAs. Instead, we like to think of the firm itself as a dynamic catalogue of learning opportunities that offer an ever-changing range of ways to challenge your brain, build experience, and add value to yourself. By pursuing our growth agenda and moving into different geographies and lines of business, we can pretty much guarantee that our people will be constantly exposed to new and different things.

However, we know that while Investcorp is full of exceptionally bright minds who can sum up a company's financial situation in seconds, we also know that we're less experienced in assessing the whole person behind the brain. Fluency in reading an Excel spreadsheet is fine, but understanding what makes people tick and addressing all the things they need to grow in their career is a skill set that can always be strengthened. And it's one we should apply everywhere: internally *and* externally, among our own team leaders, and when we build relationships with the management teams of our portfolio companies.

We have plenty of IQ; as we grow, we *all* need to nurture our EQ (emotional intelligence) abilities. That's one of the reasons I encourage our high-potential people to engage a personal coach, whom Investcorp pays for. Coaching is a reliable way to identify blind spots in how we engage with others and, more important, offer solutions.

I also try to model the behavior I'd like to see more of. For example, people like to be listened to, so I try to set an example by listening to everyone. I encourage people to contact me if they have a question about something. Every quarter, I ask our Human Resources folks for a list of new joiners, and I make sure to have a one-on-one meeting with each one. They are the next generation, and the generation after that at Investcorp, so it's very important to encourage their inputs, get them energized, and make them feel they are the future of the firm.

When people feel they are part of making things happen, they get more involved and are more engaged. To accomplish that means assigning them to work on different projects, inviting junior people to join committees and conference calls, and asking them to do things they've never done before. It means demonstrating that we genuinely want to learn from different generations and geographies and genders by instituting reverse-mentoring and partnering with senior leaders.

We're already doing this, but we know we can do more. To reflect the future, we have to adapt today. If we don't, we won't attract the right talent that will ensure we *have* a future.

CHALLENGE: MAINTAINING OUR CULTURE

Here's a startling statistic: over 60 percent of Investcorp's employees have been with the firm for fewer than five years; more than 40 percent joined in the past three years; and 25 percent joined in the past year alone. That may be nothing in a tech start-up, but it's a huge amount of new talent for a forty-year-old investment management firm.

Here's another interesting fact: the standard turnover rate in this industry is close to 20 percent. Our turnover rate is confidential, but I can attest that we have very low turnover compared to our peers.

In other words, our high percentage of new people is almost entirely due to our growth. But while people come for the growth opportunity, they stay because of our culture.

What is culture? Basically, it's a set of agreed-upon behaviors of how we're going to interact with each other and with our entire ecosystem: clients, partners, shareholders—even competitors.

We're constantly measured on our performance: that's *the* most important benchmark when serving our investors and clients. What we deliver in terms of returns is one number you cannot escape from. However, *how* we achieve our results is as important as how well we perform. We're like a sports team: there's high individual accountability, but we have to come together and play cohesively. We have to win to ensure we have a future. But we have to win the right way.

The Investcorp culture is idiosyncratic in the industry. "People help each other," said Andrea Davis, head of Corporate Strategy. "In other firms, you eat only what you kill, and that changes the culture massively. Here, it's a learning culture. I feel I can take risks and develop."

We begin by recruiting people who are not only smart but also naturally curious. Then we force-feed that curiosity by constantly asking them questions and soliciting their views. This is a competitive business, and people want to contribute. If you know you're going into a meeting at which you'll be asked for your opinion, you'll quickly sharpen your curiosity.

We try to satisfy that curiosity through a culture that's open to new ideas. I'm happy to consider any idea that makes sense. That's both my job and my inclination, although sometimes the idea stream can be overwhelming.

Our road map serves as the filtering system; there are lots of different ways to achieve our goal of $100 billion AUM, but the road map helps us decide what we should and shouldn't be doing, and whether we should do it now or put it off for a better time. It's vitally important to always— *always*—explain why we can't do these things or can't do them now, so that people understand that their ideas have value, even if we don't implement them. The last thing we want is for people to feel dismissed.

Hand in hand with fostering a learning culture is promoting a collaborative culture. One of the biggest challenges, when I became Executive

Chairman eight years ago, was bridging and breaking down silos, as I described in chapter 4. The silos still exist—to a lesser degree, I'm happy to say—but our growth has helped to dissolve them. The more global we become, the more opportunities emerge for cross-function connections.

For example, in 2021, Walid Majdalani, who at the time was in charge of finding investment opportunities for us in the Middle East and North Africa, learned that NoorNet, the largest privately owned internet service provider in Saudi Arabia, was up for sale. It was a great opportunity for us. The only hitch was that the price tag was a little too big for our private equity purse. Rather than look outside for co-investors, though, Hazem Ben-Gacem had the idea of partnering with Investcorp's own technology investment team in a 50/50 split, as the opportunity also sat neatly within the technology fund's remit. "Walid's team brought in geographical expertise and my team brought sector knowhow," recalled Gilbert Kamieniecky, who leads our technology team. NoorNet was the first investment in our Technology Fund V.

We're increasingly collaborating across global groups, combining horizontal country expertise and vertical sector expertise. That enables us to take a more global approach in these special sectors. When we learn about new tech trends in the United States, we can predict what might happen in Europe, the Middle East, and Asia, and then we apply that knowledge to our investment products.

Even as we grow globally, we remain a one-firm culture. We're not a Middle Eastern firm, we're not a U.S. firm, nor are we an Indian firm. "The firm's culture trumps any local culture," noted Rishi Kapoor. "That unanimity of opinion—it's a huge differentiator."

The challenge is how to preserve and disseminate the culture when we're growing so quickly. Paradoxically, our success carries the seeds of its greatest threat: "Our business is a people-based business," Rishi said. "With all the new people being onboarded, you run the risk of potentially eroding the cultural identity that defines the firm. As we grow, we may become more siloed. Businesses may be less willing to cross-pollinate ideas. Hubris can set in. Success makes you relax. And there's no room for relaxation."

Fortunately, we can recognize the symptoms of the disease. Even more fortunately, we have the antibodies. We continually acculturate our new employees—and remind our existing ones—by constantly reiterating our vision and reinforcing the pathways we're taking to realize that vision. Only so much is absorbed each time, so you have to update the message regularly with new and different examples. We have done that multiple times, and we will no doubt continue to do it many more times. The day we stop is the day we stop growing.

In addition, we periodically examine our culture and ask ourselves, *What do we stand for? What is important? What is relevant today? What will no longer be relevant tomorrow?* Even as we evolve, there will always be some key elements we want to retain: being a learning culture, being willing to question the status quo, and wanting to welcome new ideas.

We need to hardwire adaptability into our culture if we're to survive another forty years.

CHALLENGE: SCALING UP OUR BUSINESS

In 2015, when I became Executive Chairman, we created a road map for growth and took the first steps on our journey. Since then, we've expanded into new geographies, introduced new lines of business, launched new investment platforms, and acquired a new set of clients. But will these accomplishments be enough? I don't think so.

I think we are at an inflection point. Thanks to our acquisition of Marble Point Credit Management in January 2023 (more about this later), we're halfway to our goal of $100 billion in AUM. We can certainly continue to bolt on additional geographies or asset classes. But incremental growth alone won't be what gets us to where we want to be. How can we grow our platforms even more? How can we make a quantum leap?

We need to scale up massively.

In chapter 5, I described the advantages of increasing scale. A brief recap: Scaling up gives you muscles. In times of trouble, you have the ability to bounce back because you're big enough to withstand the hits. This also enables you to do so much more with the same cost base. Growth alone is costly: you have to buy new businesses, hire more people, open more offices. Growth alone can make you too big and cumbersome. Greater scale, on the other hand, pushes existing businesses to look for innovative ways to attract additional capital and forces you to be nimble.

Scaling up is not limited to one methodology. You can do it in two ways: organically or inorganically. Either you acquire a business or you develop an existing one. Since 2015, we've done both. Now we have to figure out how to leverage those businesses even more.

One way we've scaled up organically is in our real estate business. The historic constraint on that particular platform was that investor capital was limited to our traditional sources. Back in 2015, if you had said to the real estate folks, "We want you to attract institutional money," they wouldn't have known where to start. But when that became the target for the entire firm, they pitched in and learned how to do it.

Our real estate platform used to be structured with an investment/acquisition team and an asset management team. The investment team assessed potential deals and bought the properties, then they turned them over to the management team. The acquisition people tended to be generalists, working across asset classes ranging from industrial facilities to residential housing, which itself was spread among purpose-built student accommodations (PBSA) and multi-family dwellings (also known as a "shared house" or a "house in multiple occupation," or HMO).

To become more attractive to institutional capital and to grow, the group split into two vertical lines of business: half now concentrates on buying and managing industrial and logistics properties and half focuses on residential real estate. "You're not talking about residential assets one day and commercial another day," explained Mike O'Brien, who oversees the residential portfolio while his colleague, Herb Myers, looks after the commercial side. "Now we're each hyper-focused on our own specific asset class."

Our timing was fortuitous. Historically, institutional investors under-weighted housing and warehouses—known in real estate lingo as "beds, heads, and sheds"—preferring to put their money into shopping centers and office buildings (the traditional definition of "commercial real estate"). As it turned out, those were the two asset classes that got hit hardest during the COVID pandemic. Meanwhile, we happened to become special-ists in the two asset classes that were turbocharged during COVID; think of all the people who were relocating from cities in California and along the East Coast to the Sun Belt, as well as the massive need for warehouse space as a result of the growth in e-commerce.

"Scalability really put us on the map," observed Herb Myers. "Within a relatively short time of splitting into verticals, we landed two sizable institutional investors from blue-chip sovereign wealth funds in Asia. Real estate had never raised institutional capital on that scale before. Now we continue to springboard off of that to do more."

We've been following a similar strategy of "beds, heads, sheds, and meds"—(HMOs, PBSAs, industrial and logistics space, and increasingly, biotech facilities)—in Europe and India. Meanwhile, to further focus our expertise where it can do the most good, we partnered with Titan, a U.S. real estate investment manager specializing in residential homes and multi-family dwellings. By letting them do what they do best, we can do what we do best.

If what we've done in real estate is an example of scaling up organi-cally, our acquisition of Marble Point Credit Management in early 2023 is an example of doing it inorganically.

Acquiring Marble Point was not scale simply for the sake of scale. It's scaling smartly, by filling in areas where we had a gap. For us, Marble Point brought on board as strong a credit business in the United States as Jeremy Ghose had developed for 3i in Europe and Japan. We're not just scaling up the overall number but scaling in the right way in the right space. That, to me, was the most important thing strategically.

In addition to Marble Point's own $7.8 billion in assets under management—which, when combined with Investcorp's own credit management business, brings our total AUM in this line of business to $22 billion and raises our rank to among the top fifteen CLO managers globally by AUM—we're also bringing on board human talent. Much of what Marble Point had in terms of capabilities and relationships was different from what Investcorp already had. Just like when we bought IDFC in India, the Marble Point acquihire was additive. Not incidentally, the acquisition of Marble Point put our own total AUM over $50 billion.

Another way to scale up is to leverage our existing capital by investing it in a different way. One of our recent successes is our GP stakes business. (I described this a little in chapter 9, in the context of our diversity efforts.) A GP stakes investment is the direct acquisition of a minority equity position, or stake, in an alternative asset manager (the General Partner, or GP), either directly or through a specialized fund that builds a portfolio of GP stakes. It's become a popular strategy in recent years because it gives investors a share of the returns from what may be multiple funds managed by the firm, and consequently, brings the advantage of diversification. And it's a scalable business because you don't need additional resources for each fund.

What we like about GP staking is that it's similar to private equity, but it differs in two significant ways: it produces an annual dividend stream plus, eventually, a capital gain, both of which boost our AUM; and the investing horizon is much longer than the typical five-year private equity limit. That makes GP staking a strategy that's especially attractive to institutional investors and, increasingly, to other parts of the private market.

As always, we continue to focus on our sweet spot: the middle market. We believe that mid-sized GPs represent a compelling opportunity because that's where the greatest potential for growth is.[2]

GP staking is a fairly new business and it continues to evolve, but there's no doubt about the growth potential for us. While we struggled to raise purely institutional capital investment vehicles, Investcorp Strategic Capital Partners raised more than $800 million for its inaugural GP stakes fund from institutional investors and some limited partners right out of the gate. (The target was $750 million.) Consequently, we're launching Fund II much sooner than we ever thought we would, and at a larger size.

We've spent over forty years investing in the middle market and we know it intimately. We know how to help mid-sized firms grow into major enterprises; they know they wouldn't last for long if they didn't. Now we have to apply that thinking to ourselves. We have to scale up if we want to survive.

CHALLENGE: EXPLORING NEW SOURCES OF CAPITAL

When I became Executive Chairman, Investcorp had one source of capital: private wealth in the Gulf. Then, we decided to transform ourselves to attract institutional investors. Our next step is to open a third channel and offer private market products to mass-affluent retail clients: that is, individual investors at the upper end of the mass market who aren't quite as wealthy as our traditional high-net-worth clients. It's part of a larger story in how to diversify sources of capital and provide a wider range of offerings to a broader spectrum of investors.

"One of the most intriguing trends in investing today is the democratization of private equity. A new generation of mass-affluent investors is far more knowledgeable about investing," said Yusef Al Yusef, who is heading up our private wealth initiative. "They realize that private market investments can complement their asset allocation strategy, diversify the risk of investing solely in public markets, and add alpha [an industry term for exceeding benchmark returns] over the medium term."

In the past, accessing private markets was restricted to ultra-wealthy investors, whom we served through our traditional face-to-face model.

Building and maintaining the relationship was extraordinarily time-consuming. The relationship manager would schedule a meeting with the client. They'd sit down, drink a coffee, discuss the offering, and shake hands. The manager would return to the office and print out the relevant documents. Then he'd schedule another meeting, go back to the client, drink another coffee, discuss the offering, and so on. During the pitch to acquire Tyrrells Potato Crisps, Abdul Rahim Saad, our head of global partnerships, joked that he shared so many product samples with prospective investors that he gained ten pounds.

There's simply no way we could maintain that model if we wanted to grow.

Today, those in-person visits can be optimized by technology. Now that investors are accustomed to living in the digital era, they don't expect you to physically be there as much—nor do they want you to be. Their grandfather or father was accustomed to leisurely face-to-face conversations, but many in today's generation would prefer to see a ten-minute video on their phone or iPad, or to open the Investcorp Private Wealth app, rather than flip through a 160-slide deck.

These shifts in demography and technology further accelerate the democratization of private equity. While we don't intend for a relationship to be replaced by a bot, our digital interface can support and streamline decision-making. And with more efficient ways to access products and data, investment strategies can be made available for a much lower cost, lowering the bar for investors and expanding the pool of potential clients.

We've already been partnering with private banks in Europe, registered investment advisors (RIAs) in the United States, and similar wealth aggregators around the world who can provide a conduit for their clients to access our private equity offerings. Launching an app will further enable us to tap the multi-billion-dollar global wealth market without the expense of opening offices and building teams. "The app has the potential to be downloaded by a mass-affluent investor from the Gulf or Europe, or Southeast Asia," Yusef noted. "We're perfectly positioned to leverage the firm's brand name and resources to cater to the needs of the mass-affluent in the Gulf and potentially the world."

Another way to tap different streams of capital is through special-purpose acquisition companies (SPACs). Also known as a "blank-check company," a SPAC is a shell corporation that's listed on a stock exchange for the sole and special purpose of acquiring a private company within a certain amount of time, usually two years. Once the SPAC has bought the company, that company automatically lists on the stock exchange without having to go through the minutiae of a tradition initial public offering process.

SPACs first appeared in the 1990s as a creative way to work around a U.S. prohibition on listing blank-check companies. For years, SPACs had a questionable reputation owing to a lack of strict regulation. With increased focus from the Securities and Exchange Commission ensuring more regulation, however, SPACs soared in popularity. The New York Stock Exchange launched its first SPAC in May 2017.[3] More recently, 2021 saw over 600 SPACs listed on the NYSE and NASDAQ.[4]

One of those SPACs was sponsored by us. We looked at the booming SPAC market and asked ourselves, *How can firms with no track record raise hundreds of millions of dollars? There's room for professionals, and that's us.* Our debut was a sponsored European SPAC—Investcorp Europe Acquisition Corporation I—listed on the NASDAQ on December 19, 2021. We celebrated its launch by ringing the opening bell on March 23, 2022.

SPACs are a bridge to two different investor classes. Institutional investors provide the initial capital. After we find the target company and list it on a public exchange, it then becomes accessible to retail investors. Even though the number of SPAC listings dropped in 2022, we believe SPACs are here to stay. The number of public companies has decreased dramatically over the past two decades, even as the amount of money flowing into the public markets has increased. At the same time, there has been a surge in the amount of capital invested in private equity. All this money is looking for an outlet.

Investcorp, perhaps more than any other private equity firm, is especially well suited for sponsoring SPACs, for two reasons. "Because a SPAC buys only one business at a time, SPACs are essentially deal-by-deal transactions," explained Abdul Rahim Saad. "Deal-by-deal is in our DNA."

It takes a lot of trust for an investor to hand over their money to a "blank-check company," not knowing what kind of company will be acquired. That's where Investcorp's reputation comes in. We're leveraging our credibility. With forty years of successful investment in mid-market private companies, we know how to identify promising acquisitions. That's why our first SPAC, originally subscribed at $250 million, was oversubscribed and eventually listed at $345 million.

SPACs do not lead to increases in scale. They have the potential to provide transaction fees if they find an acquisition target before the expiration date of the SPAC, but they don't measurably enhance your AUM. They are, instead, a different way of connecting both institutional capital and retail investors to regions and markets, while maximizing adjacencies that make sense for us. They boost our profile in the market, which in turn puts us on the radar screen of a larger number of potential investors. And they enable the SPAC to potentially acquire large-cap companies of over $1 billion, rather than our identifying and executing, as principal, upon opportunities in our usual sub–$1 billion ballpark.

We've already raised $225 million for our second sponsored SPAC, Investcorp India Acquisition Corp. As the market evolves, Investcorp must pivot to capture new opportunities. That's something I think about a lot. We have to keep exploring these areas of growth and find ways to make them attractive to private, retail, and institutional investors. This is what will provide us with the capital to scale up.

CHALLENGE: SHARPENING SITUATIONAL AWARENESS

When you play at the global level, you have to develop a broader perspective. You have to know about politics and policy, the rich and the poor, and the left and right of society. Otherwise, it's like wearing glacier goggles when you're climbing a mountain: you only see the peak in front of you, not the crevasses on either side.

I always want to consider the whole ecosystem: the government, the financial sector, the media, and the public and private sectors. It's amazing what you can triangulate from that data, how you can connect ideas that you can then use to advise people or help your business. When you gather intelligence from multiple disciplines, you open not just the doors but also the windows. You get a much wider range of inputs and viewpoints.

The challenge is how to spread that wider perspective throughout the firm to sharpen everyone's situational awareness. Investcorp's own organizational structure and culture promote different points of view. The fact that we have two co-CEOs is a start. Rishi and Hazem would be the first to say they don't always agree, but that their divergent opinions are a good thing. "We challenge each other," Hazem said, "then we have a third person who's the ultimate arbiter."

That's my role. And just to be clear, I weigh in on strategic issues. I leave investment decisions to the investment committees.

Similarly, we encourage independent thinking throughout the firm, from the Executive Committee and the Operating Committee to each business's investment committee and so on. Everyone has the right to share their opinion—in fact, we expect them to share it. Encouraging a diversity of opinions and intellectual dissent is how you avoid blind spots and groupthink, and you get to see things from different angles. It's a learning opportunity.

Investcorp has always welcomed outside expertise. Calling on experts is another way of learning. What's key is to have a wide range of experts, not just "the usual suspects." The more brains to pick and the greater the diversity of thought, the better.

Everywhere I go—even when I go digitally, rather than physically—I try to meet people who are in the market, whose companies are ahead of us and are bigger than we are. Because they're bigger and have been in business longer than we have, they see things we may not see. They're exposed in ways we're not—yet. They can validate what we're doing and, more important, we can learn from them.

Our co-CEOs and I constantly study other investment firms to see how they gather and deploy their assets to boost their own growth. That's how we decided to move into the insurance advisory business.

We noticed that Apollo Global Management, an American-based alternative asset management firm, had bought a $12 million stake in a life insurance company that, in ten years, grew from a firm smaller than we were to have more than $300 billion in AUM. Their idea was that, by investing a portion of the insurer's assets in alternative assets, including in private equity, the insurer could receive higher returns on their capital, on which Apollo could, in turn, charge management fees. At a time of historically low interest rates, the idea attracted some of the other big PE firms—KKR and Blackstone, among others—to follow suit.

We were attracted to the idea, too.

Insurance is intrinsically a business built to scale up: the more capital an insurance company has, the more fixed annuity policies it can issue. A fixed annuity is basically a way for people to create their own pension. A person gives an insurance company a certain amount of money up front, in return for a guaranteed stream of income to be delivered over a determined period of time. The risk in delivering that fixed rate of return lies with the insurance company. Typically, the majority of those assets are put into government bonds and more secure investments to meet that obligation, with a portion invested according to a predetermined and regulated risk level to try to generate additional returns.

In the United States alone, Americans pay more than $200 billion every year in annuity premiums to supplement their pensions and Social Security checks.[5] We liked the steady growth that advising insurance companies could potentially provide to our AUM, as well as the opportunity to potentially support insurers to offer annuity holders the potentially higher yield that alternative assets can provide compared to conventional public equities and bonds.

In October 2021, Investcorp announced the creation of our own Insurance Solutions platform to provide investment management services to insurers such as Sunset Life Insurance Company of America. (It's since been renamed Ibexis.) Ibexis is focused, like other insurance companies, on offering fixed index annuities to its customers, a $112 billion market[6] being driven by demographics, with 10,000 baby boomers reaching retirement age every day. "We hope, as its advisor, to manage Ibexis's assets and, where relevant, draw upon all the things that Investcorp is really good at," explained Todd Fonner, the Chief Investment Officer of the platform. "We'll allocate the Ibexis portfolio as required to ensure that it meets its targeted risk/return criteria, which will include an exposure to the sorts of alternative, private capital assets that firms like Investcorp manage. It's a model that I believe has the right balance of capabilities and alignment of interests."

Dave Tayeh liked to joke that in his early days with Investcorp people often confused us with Invesco, the Denver-based insurance company. He'd have to explain that, no, Investcorp was an asset management company. But now we're in the insurance advisory business, too, all because of keeping our eyes and ears open.

And speaking of keeping our eyes and ears open, wherever I go I try to talk with young people. They give me a fresh perspective about a place. If I see excited young entrepreneurs who are able to turn their ideas into something tangible, that's a great indication that the country and economy are doing the right things. If I find that the young people are unmotivated and unenthusiastic, then I know there is a problem.

I'm always looking to make connections that will help Investcorp, by expanding both my own perspective and that of our people. When I attend the World Economic Forum in Davos, for example, or summits at the Milken Institute, I'm only one person. (I always invite key executives to join me, but many of the most fruitful connections arise from serendipitous one-on-one encounters, such as the dinner conversation with Gerry Grimstone I described in chapter 7.) But I can serve as a "force multiplier" by inviting the experts I meet to be guest speakers at OpCom and ExCom meetings, investor conferences, and our town halls. This connects people in the firm with world leaders whom they'd otherwise never have a chance to talk to.

We try to bring in people who are from outside our world but who are relevant to our business or to the political or economic situation. They provide a high-level perspective while also helping us see and think about things differently. As I described in chapter 10, Mohamed El-Erian warned us about the impact of the COVID pandemic before the World Health Organization declared it a global health emergency. His red flag gave us a small but crucial head start in preparing our response.

Hosting people like Michael Milken, former Greek Minister of Finance Yanis Varoufakis, former U.S. National Security Advisor Stephen Hadley, former Chief of the U.K. Defence Staff General David Richards, and Sophie Pedder, Paris bureau chief for *The Economist* and author of *Revolution Française: Emmanuel Macron and the Quest to Reinvent a Nation*, is great for our brand, for how people feel about the firm. It gives them a lot of confidence when they can mingle with and ask questions of such successful leaders. And it sharpens everyone's situational awareness: these people will always be more experienced than us and better informed, so we always learn something.

Another crucial influence in my "continuing education" is my participation in the Eisenhower Fellowship and the Brookings Institution. The Eisenhower Fellowship, where I'm on the board of trustees, identifies innovative future leaders from all over the world; each year, it selects forty to fifty mid-career high-achievers in the fields most critical to their home countries' needs and brings them to the United States for six weeks of intensive professional exploration, interaction, and exchange with experts in their fields. The Fellowship also does this on a smaller scale with their American counterparts. You can just imagine the excitement and enthusiasm, not to mention all the ideas, when all this brainpower gets together. It's a program I'm really proud to be associated with.

The Brookings Institution—well, what can I say? It's one of the greatest think tanks in the world. You go to one of their semi-annual conferences for two or three days, and you're briefed about everything that's happening in the world, from the people who are shaping the policies and putting them into action. The caliber of intellect associated with the Brookings is unbelievable. Plus, I like the excuse to go back to Washington, D.C., where I lived when I was at the National Defense University.

I encourage our people to create their own connections, too. Engaging with their peers in the marketplace, talking with investors, attending industry conferences like the Future Investment Initiative in Riyadh and the SuperReturn International enables them to find out what other people are thinking and exposes them to new ideas. It expands their point of view and sharpens their situational awareness.

Situational awareness is not only about your ability to perceive what's happening around you. A key element also involves shaping your own situation: your position in the universe in which you operate and how that affects others' perceptions of you.

In 2021, we took a giant step in our metamorphosis by delisting from the Bahrain Stock Exchange. We had been listed on the Bahrain bourse for almost four decades, starting at a time when Bahrain was the financial center of the Middle East. However, trading on the Bahrain exchange has languished in recent years. On some days, fewer than 1 million shares change hands overall. Investcorp shares might be traded once a month and a mere $5,000 trade could move our stock price 10 percent. We're proud of our roots in Bahrain, but our global growth strategy required more liquidity than the local stock exchange could provide.

Delisting and becoming a private company enabled us to focus single-mindedly on building the business and pursuing a growth strategy the Investcorp way: deliberately and with a long-term perspective. We didn't want to be hampered by having to hit certain benchmarks every quarter; we wanted the independence and adaptability to make the many tough decisions that face us on our growth journey. We're fortunate that our shareholders understand the trade-off between short-term gains and long-term value, and they support our strategy. They, like us, are in it for the long haul. As a result, we're in a different and stronger position to shape our future.

///

We're in the business of being worried every day. When you are on a growth journey, doing different things in different markets, there's always something that's going to affect your business. There's always a new challenge to confront. I'm delighted that we surpassed our goal of $50 billion in AUM, but that doesn't mean we should sit back and relax.

When I think about our future, the biggest and most threatening risk—the one that encompasses the five challenges described in this chapter—is the risk of missing opportunities.

Ice hockey great Wayne Gretzky famously said, "I skate to where the puck is going, not to where it's been." But there's more to scoring a success than knowing where the puck is going. It's being able to figure it out before your competitors do and get there faster.

That's what I mean about developing the right muscles and training ourselves to use them. The more we can combine agility and ability, the better the chance we'll be in the right place at the right time with the team with the right skills. It takes a lot of practice and a fair amount of luck.

There's another saying from another sports legend that speaks directly to that. The story goes that when golf icon Jack Nicklaus hit his eighteenth hole-in-one, a fan congratulated him on his good luck. Nicklaus thanked him and replied, "The more I practice, the luckier I get."

I said earlier that I believe you can make your own luck. I believe that every day provides an opportunity to practice: to strengthen existing skills and learn and leverage new ones that will help us withstand future shocks. Every day, we can work to increase the likelihood that things will tilt our way. When we have confidence in our strategy and our tactics, every challenge is another stage in our transformation, another step in our journey to connect to the future.

THE PROMISE OF PRIVATE CAPITAL

I n 2015, when I was asked to become Executive Chairman of Investcorp, one of the main factors that convinced me to say yes was the opportunity to make a difference and do good things in the world.

I realize that may sound at odds with an industry often portrayed as prioritizing personal financial gains above all else. And certainly there are a lot of people who come into this business because they just want to make a lot of money, without thinking about how they make it.

I would hope, however, that's not the reason they choose to work at Investcorp. Because I believe that private markets can do so much more. And I believe that because of Investcorp's approach to private markets, we have the potential to make a meaningful social, cultural, and economic impact in the world.

THE POWER OF PRIVATE EQUITY

Let's start with private equity, the foundation of Investcorp's business. Private equity is the business of investing equity capital in private companies, with the hope of ultimately increasing the value of that stake. Companies seed prosperity: they provide employment, they strengthen communities, and they nurture creativity. If you look at what built the

U.S. economy, the largest in the world, you'll see that it's all the companies that were started or found a home there.

Although public companies tend to hog the news headlines, private companies are the true dynamos for value creation. In the United States alone, in 2021, there were approximately 17,500 private companies with annual revenues greater than $100 million, compared to roughly 2,600 public companies above the same revenue threshold.[1] Outside of the United States, there are approximately 2,800 public companies with revenues greater than $100 million, compared to 18,000 private companies of that size.[2] On a global scale, private equity invested $512 billion in buyout deal value in the first half of 2022 alone, compared with $179.5 billion in capital raised from IPO listings in all of 2022.[3]

Investcorp originally established a niche in mid-market private companies for a simple reason: as growth investors, we look for companies with the potential for long-term, above-market growth. In the United States in particular, there are many more mid-market companies than there are large companies, so there are more investment opportunities to explore. Fewer than 15 percent of U.S. companies with revenues over $100 million are publicly held, limiting the opportunity for public investors to participate in the broader economy.[4] Investcorp's sweet spot is generally between $200 million and $1 billion of total enterprise value, which includes both equity and debt. In other words, these companies tend to be well established, without the risks associated with a start-up. They are poised and eager to grow.

And we can do so much to help them achieve their ambitions. You've heard the comment that it's easier to turn a battleship than a supertanker. (It's true. Just for the record, a supertanker has a turning radius of approximately 2 kilometers, while a battleship needs only 700 yards.) We chose—and continue to choose—to specialize in this area because we can make a much greater impact on a mid-market firm than on a large-cap behemoth.

When we acquire or invest in a company, our goal is long-term value creation: we want to take a good business and help make it better for all its constituents—its shareholders, employees, customers, and vendors. That's why we prefer to buy a controlling share or a substantial minority investment; we have more influence over the growth strategy. We look for mid-sized, services-focused companies with strong management teams and solid cash flows—firms that occupy a prominent place in their industry and have a rich potential for growth. We identify a company's seeds of greatness—what makes it special—and use the expertise gleaned from overseeing the scores of similar companies in our portfolio to nurture those seeds and help the company achieve its fullest potential during our time together.

Our growth strategy particularly resonates with family businesses whose owners are ready to retire and don't have a designated heir, or founder-led firms whose founders are looking for outside advice and capital to help the firm grow. In both cases, rather than break the company up, we boost and build upon what they started. We act as a strategic partner, drawing on our forty years of experience, as well as on Investcorp's network of actively engaged advisory directors and independent board directors, all of whom are seasoned executives with highly successful track records in their respective fields. We provide a wealth of expertise that simply would not be available to most companies of this size.

We also look for "corporate orphans"—smaller companies that were acquired by larger conglomerates but were sidelined after a change of leadership or strategy. When the focus shifts to the core businesses that are seen as the organization's future, these orphans are ignored and neglected, starved of capital and management resources, until they're eventually sold off. That's what happened with Tiffany, the luxury jewelers, which Avon bought in 1979, only to put it on the block five years later after deciding it wanted to concentrate on the beauty, direct mail, and healthcare products that constituted some 96 percent of its sales.[5] Investcorp bought it in 1984 and three years later, took it public at a profit estimated to be at least $100 million.[6]

Our aim is to find companies that are leaders in fragmented industries. The mid-market is a particularly good place to play because it's so dynamic. Our key value add is to provide the institutional platform: appropriate sales, marketing, and finance functions; upgraded digital and IT; a streamlined management and organizational structure; proper governance; ESG guidance. That enables these companies to scale up and expand through acquisitions of their own, further consolidating the industry around them.

When it's time to sell a company in our portfolio, I would estimate that 70 percent of the returns we generate come through activities that have improved the company and have added value.

In chapter 10, I described how we did that with Fortune Fish & Gourmet, but that's just one of many examples. Others include American Tire, which we bought for $700 million and sold five years later for $1.3 billion; the Wrench Group, which when we bought it provided essential home maintenance and repair services in four markets in the United States, and three years later, when we sold it, had expanded to seven major markets; and United Talent Agency (UTA), which, in its three years under our wings, more than tripled its EBITDA through exceptional organic growth and several strategic acquisitions. These are just examples in North America. We apply the same formula in Europe, India, the Middle East, and the other geographies where we operate.

Private equity has a bad reputation for buying companies and destroying them, liquidating businesses, selling off assets, sacking employees, or drowning companies with impossible amounts of debt. (In 2005, German politician Franz Müntefering famously denounced private equity firms as "swarms of locusts that fall on companies, stripping them bare before moving on."7) That approach is ultimately not healthy—for people, for companies, for the communities they operate in, or for society as a whole. It may produce short-term profits, but over the long-term it inevitably results in the destruction of value.

We aim to create value. We support a model that preserves businesses, promotes growth, and creates jobs. I think without the interjection of good private equity, a lot of companies would wither or just disappear. By shaping and strengthening them, we can offer them a robust new life.

That's our responsibility and we embrace it. But that's just the first step.

A LEVER FOR TRANSFORMATION

Over the past few years we have embraced another responsibility. As Investcorp has grown beyond private equity to encompass the wider world of private capital—credit management, a markedly expanded real estate portfolio, strategic capital, infrastructure investments, and an insurance advisory unit—we are seizing the opportunity to fulfill the broader promise of private markets: to be a lever for transformation on a large scale.

Every one of the decisions we make involves a choice. As I described in chapter 9, increasingly that choice involves strengthening our mission of sustainability. Being serious about sustainability means seeding responsible stewardship throughout every aspect of our business: the companies in our private equity portfolios; the real estate properties we own and operate; the support to minority- and women-owned businesses we provide through GP staking; the partnerships we enter into; the credit we extend. All these elements promote further growth the right way: They promote growth that is good for the company, good for our employees and customers, and good for the communities we operate in.

That's how we operate in our own microcosm. But we also operate in a macrocosm, the large universe of private markets. We send a message to that universe by how and where we choose to invest. Our actions can make a difference because of the intrinsic nature of private markets.

Private markets offer advantages that public markets can't supply. One of the most significant difference is that whereas public markets can be fickle and impatient, private markets provide the luxury of a longer time frame. You can build a private business the right way, without investors insisting on quarter-over-quarter profits.

Governments are also a source of funding that takes a long view, but accessing government funds too often involves complicated approval processes, as well as thrashing through forests of red tape. Private markets are much more nimble. And privately managed projects have a greater likelihood of coming in on time and on budget.

That's why, in fact, governments are increasingly turning to public-private partnerships, especially with regard to infrastructure investments, the backbone of an economy. And that's why we've gotten involved in this field.

Infrastructure investment is a hybrid between investing in real estate and private equity, Investcorp core competencies going back to the 1980s. A natural evolution from where we started, it has developed into its own asset class—one that is intrinsically longer term than either real estate and private equity. Because infrastructure investing is governed by long-term contracts that, when governments are the client, guarantee more certain revenues, it drives more stable and predictable returns—elements that are particularly attractive to institutional investors.

Our joint venture with Aberdeen Standard (now abrdn) answers the need for improved social infrastructure in the Gulf region. Through that fund, we intend to help build modern hospitals, more schools, and address the shortage of affordable housing.

But the need for improved infrastructure is a global phenomenon, especially as roads, railways, ports, and airports built a generation ago require upgrades to satisfy tomorrow's demands. Consequently, we are actively looking for ways to expand and enhance our involvement with this asset class through future partnerships and investments around the world.

Where the promise of private markets shines brightest, however, is in the areas it can identify and explore for investment well before public markets and governments are ready to commit capital. Consider Amazon, Google, Apple, and Facebook. These four companies have fundamentally changed all our lives. The initial funding for all four came from private market capital.

Today, Investcorp is looking into companies whose products and services will address the most pressing demographic, technological, environmental, and geopolitical issues that will shape the global economy in the next three decades. To help structure our strategy, every year since 2019, in partnership with the International Institute for Management Development (IMD), we poll global institutional investors on their sentiments and allocations regarding the most pressing megatrends. Then we compile their responses into an annual survey, "What's Next? Investment Trends for the Future." We take these findings into account when we analyze the implications of current and future investment opportunities.

For example, among the top ten global trends identified in our 2023 survey are: digitization and artificial intelligence (AI); an aging population; food security; improving healthcare delivery; decarbonization and the transition to net zero; the near-shoring and re-shoring of supply chains; and increasing urbanization.

We're already investing in companies that will enable a wave of innovation in many of these areas for years to come. Take supply-chain management. We're not just improving the quality of the "sheds" that distribution companies rely on; we're also involved in the logistics that move the goods in and out of those warehouses more efficiently. Consider improving healthcare delivery. Since our initial investment in NephroPlus in 2019, the India-based chain of dialysis services has expanded to more than 300 centers across India, the Philippines, Uzbekistan, and other countries in East and West Asia.

Digitization is an especially powerful wave, with the potential to re-shape our lives in ways we can barely imagine. We believe that blockchain technology will transform every facet of our economy, much as the internet did in the 2000s. That's why in April 2022, we launched a new global fund investing in companies operating in the blockchain ecosystem. It wasn't an obvious focus for a fund, but our thought was that by investing in companies with an established business model and proven market fit, and by working with their founders, we could simultaneously participate in and learn more about this fast-growing and significant sector.

What makes private equity exciting is that we can invest in companies that are still too small or too innovative to come to the public's attention. We can subsidize new ideas that could turn into the next Google, the next Amazon, the next Facebook. We can sow the seeds of the future.

And we can do it in a way that makes a difference.

Our North American real estate group recently launched a scholarship program that aims to do just that. Real estate isn't an obvious source of scholarship funding. Our thinking, though, is that we own about 25,000 apartment units in the United States, so we're directly engaged with about 50,000 people in the communities we operate in. It's not an insignificant number. Our renters tend to be hard-working people who have solid jobs, but who could use a helping hand—for themselves or for their kids—to learn a new trade skill, get a professional certification, or take the extra college classes to earn a diploma. We're happy to use some of our net profits to help them improve their lives and to invest in a future we all share.

Doing well by doing good hasn't always been associated with private markets. But I believe that can change. At the end of the day, we think that companies that provide a better service and a better product will be profitable, and by being profitable, they will raise the standards for the entire field they operate in.

At Investcorp, we push people to refine—and redefine—best business practices. The more we make it a priority, the more opportunities we have to prove it. The more we scale up, the more people will hear our message. And the more successful we are, the more likely other firms will follow our example. It won't happen overnight. It's part of a long journey. But by committing to that journey, we commit to our responsibility as a force for transformative change.

CONNECTING TO THE FUTURE

Investcorp has always been a bridge builder. We began by connecting money from the Gulf with investment opportunities in the United States and Europe. Forty years later, we're connecting global investors with opportunities to make the world a better place.

Our own growth journey since 2015 has been one of discovery and reinvention, of exploring opportunities and uncovering capabilities. I think everyone would agree that we have transformed ourselves, as a firm and as individuals. Instead of being stagnant and self-protective, we have learned to stretch, to try things the "old Investcorp" would have shunned, and to embrace ideas we would once have dismissed. We have sharpened our situational awareness to see doors where once we saw only blank walls, and we have developed the skills to open those doors and confidently walk through them. We have strengthened our muscles to lift bigger weights; each step up in scale enables us to make even more of a difference in the world.

It's a journey I've been proud to be a part of. Most of all, I've been honored and humbled by the many smart people who have committed to join that journey. Together, we can look forward to another forty years of building bridges to new worlds and connecting to the future.

ACKNOWLEDGMENTS

One of the first and most valuable lessons I learned as a young fighter pilot was that while you may be the only person in the cockpit, you are just one member of a crew. The success of a mission is due as much to them as it is to you. Similarly, *Connecting to the Future*, like Investcorp's own journey, relied on the efforts of a large and committed team.

There are many people at Investcorp who contributed their time and their thoughts to the making of this book. They start with my partners and colleagues in the firm. My sincere thanks go to (in alphabetical order): Ramzi AbdelJaber, Habib Abdur-Rahman, Jan Erik Back, Hazem Ben-Gacem, Fortune Chigwende, Laura Coquis, Andrea Davis, Jonathan Dracos, Ebrahim Ebrahim, Todd Fonner, Jeremy Ghose, Neil Hasson, Mark Horncastle, Gilbert Kamieniecky, Rishi Kapoor, Richard Kramer, Daniel Lopez-Cruz, Walid Majdalani, Anthony Maniscalco, Michael O'Brien, Herbert Myers, Najib Rahal, Peter Rommeney, Abdulrahim Saad, Jordana Semaan, David Tayeh, Savio Tung, and Yusef Al Yusef, all of whom generously shared their recollections and perspectives.

I am grateful every day to Investcorp's "ground crew"—those who tirelessly work behind the scenes to organize our very busy schedules and ensure we hit our deadlines. Foremost amongst those is Lyn Fiel, ably assisted by a host of support staff, including our Corporate Communications group.

An outside perspective is as invaluable in sharpening one's situational awareness when writing a book as it is in business. Many thanks go to Advisory Board members Ann-Kristin Achleitner and Frances Townsend for their insights. A big thank you to Mohamed El-Erian, who wrote the Foreword to this book and whose wisdom has often kept us out of trouble.

Nawal Al-Hosany and Tina Byles Williams contributed helpful observations on, respectively, sustainable investing practices and the opportunities provided by diverse asset managers.

Three people especially gave so much of their time, energy, and critical thinking in helping tell this story.

Foremost amongst those is Catherine Fredman, my writing partner, whose probing questions and keen editorial instincts challenged me at every step even as her enthusiasm, persistent curiosity, and unflagging good humor made her a pleasure to work with. Her ability to follow my thought processes and capture my voice made me sound like myself—only better.

Tim Mattar worked in a wide variety of capacities in the firm during his twenty-eight years with Investcorp, before taking on a new role as editorial advisor. His deep knowledge of our history and comprehension of our business are matched only by his gift for explaining difficult concepts in a way that is easily digestible.

My warm thanks to Firas El Amine, who has been such an integral part of the long process of transforming an idea into a book and in shepherding it through to publication.

Likewise, my thanks go to Investcorp's Board of Directors, ably led by Dr. Yousef Al-Ebraheem, which has been understanding and supportive as we go through the large change in direction we have needed to undertake on our journey to $100 billion in AUM.

In addition to the Investcorp team, I also want to express my gratitude to Robert Barnett and Emily Alden, who from the beginning supported the story we wanted to tell and matched us with the perfect editorial team in Samantha Weiner and Richard Rhorer at Simon Element.

Last but not least, I would like to thank my wife and my family for their patience and understanding as we have sought to transform Investcorp. This has necessitated an intense travel schedule that has taken me around the world several times and away from them. Their support has been much appreciated.

I am very fortunate to have these people—and others too numerous to name—join me on this journey and ensure we are truly prepared to connect to the future.

NOTES

CHAPTER 1: LEARNING TO FLY

1. Mohammed Alardhi, *Arabs Unseen* (London: Bloomsbury, 2015), 2.
2. "Erik Bennett Obituary: Irish Aviator and Trusted Adviser to Sultan of Oman," *The Irish Times*, February 19, 2022, https://www.irishtimes.com/life-and-style/people/erik-bennett-obituary-irish-aviator-and-trusted-adviser-to-sultan-of-oman-1.4805292.

CHAPTER 2: THE FOUNDER'S CURSE

1. "Oil Shock of 1973–1974," Federal Reserve History (website), retrieved August 23, 2022, https://www.federalreservehistory.org/essays/oil-shock-of-1973-74.
2. Nemir Kirdar, *Need, Respect, Trust: The Memoir of a Vision* (London: Weidenfeld & Nicolson, 2013), 34.
3. Kirdar, *Need. Respect. Trust*, 37.
4. "A Guide to the Financial Crisis 10 Years Later," *Washington Post*, September 10, 2018.
5. "Investcorp Buys Manhattan Property for $1.4bn," *Arab News*, January 13, 2008, https://www.arabnews.com/node/307681.

6. "Blackstone's Gray: 'We're Very Thoughtful on the Size of the Capital,'" *PERE*, July 21, 2022, https://www.perenews.com/blackstone-readies -back-to-back-30bn-fundraises/.

7. "The Blackstone Group Reports Fourth Quarter and Full Year 2010 Results," *Businesswire*, February 3, 2011, https://www.businesswire .com/news/home/20110203005915/en/The-Blackstone-Group-Reports -Fourth-Quarter-and-Full-Year-2010-Results.

8. 2010 Investcorp Annual Report, Investcorp (website), https://www .investcorp.com/docs/uploads/investor-presentations/Complete _annual_report.pdf.

CHAPTER 3: WHY NOT $25 BILLION?

1. Nemir Kirdar, *Need, Respect, Trust: The Memoir of a Vision* (London: Weidenfeld & Nicolson, 2013), 359.

CHAPTER 5: CHANGING THE MINDSET

1. Jessy Williamson, "The New York Yankees: A Popular Team with a Large Fan Base," *T-Bones Baseball* (blog), December 25, 2022, https:// tbonesbaseball.com/the-new-york-yankees-a-popular-team-with-a -large-fan-base/.

2. "A.C. Milan for Those Who Love Football," A.C. Milan (website), accessed January 13, 2023, https://www.acmilan.com/en/club/sustain ability/ac-milan-of-those-who-love-football.

CHAPTER 6: THE FREE LUNCH IS NOW OVER

1. Cion Investments, "National Center for the Middle Market," *What Is Private Credit?*, accessed January 19, 2023, https://www.cioninvest ments.com/wp-content/uploads/What-is-Private-Credit-1.pdf.

CHAPTER 7: MAKE YOUR OWN LUCK

1. "China's Share of Global GDP Growth," World Economics Research (website), accessed October 24, 2022, https://www.worldeconomics .com/Global-Growth-Comparisons/China.aspx.

2. "Aging and Health in China," World Health Organization (website), accessed October 24, 2022, https://www.who.int/china/health-topics /ageing.

3. "Investcorp Announces the First Closing of Its Asia Food Brands Private Equity Joint Venture Vehicle," Investcorp (website), April 15, 2020, https://www.investcorp.com/investcorp-announces-the-first -closing-of-the-asia-food-brands-private-equity-vehicle/.

4. Dave Mead and Porsha Stiger, "The 2014 Plunge in Import Petroleum Prices: What Happened?" Bureau of Labor Statistics, *Beyond the Numbers* 4, no. 9 (May 2015), https://www.bls.gov/opub/btn/volume-4/pdf /the-2014-plunge-in-import-petroleum-prices-what-happened.pdf.

5. Marc Stocker, John Baffes, and Dana Vorisek, "What Triggered the Oil Price Plunge of 2014–2016 and Why It Failed to Deliver an Economic Impetus in Eight Charts," World Bank (blog), January 18, 2018, https://blogs.worldbank.org/developmenttalk/what-triggered-oil -price-plunge-2014-2016-and-why-it-failed-deliver-economic-impetus -eight-charts.

CHAPTER 9: OPTIMIZING THE GROWTH ENGINES

1. Amialya Durajraj, "Diabetes Is on the Rise in India: Is Fast Food to Blame?" *FoodTank*, June 2018, https://foodtank.com/news/2018/06 /diabetes-india-fast-food-nutrition/.

2. Ravi Prakash Jha et al., "Trends in the Diabetes Incidence and Mortality in India from 1990 to 2019," *Journal of Diabetes Metabolic Disorder* 20, no. 2 (July 5, 2021), https://pubmed.ncbi.nlm.nih.gov/34900822/.

3. "Diversity Wins: How Inclusion Matters," McKinsey & Company (website), May 19, 2020, https://www.mckinsey.com/featured-insights /diversity-and-inclusion/diversity-wins-how-inclusion-matters.

4. Sylvia Ann Hewlett et al., "Innovation, Diversity and Market Growth," Executive Summary, CoQual (Center for Talent Innovation), 2013, https://coqual.org/wp-content/uploads/2020/09/31_innovationdiver sityandmarketgrowth_keyfindings-1.pdf.

5. "What is ESG?" McKinsey & Company (website), January 30, 2023, https://www.mckinsey.com/featured-insights/mckinsey-explainers /what-is-esg.

CHAPTER 11: FUTURE-PROOFING THE FIRM

1. Tim Smart, "Study: Gen Z, Millennials Driving the 'Great Resignation,'" *US News & World Report*, August 26, 2021, https://www .usnews.com/news/economy/articles/2021-08-26/study-gen-z -millennials-driving-the-great-resignation.

2. Anthony Maniscalco, "The Case for Minority Investing in Mid-Size Private Capital GPs," *Investcorp Insights*, May 2020, https://www.invest corp.com/wp-content/uploads/2020/05/ISCG_The-Case-for-Minority -Equity-Investing-in-Private-Capital-GPs_White-Paper-FINAL.pdf.

3. Bob Pisani, "An Unusual 'Blank Check Company' Just Began Trading on the NYSE for the First Time Ever," CNBC (website), May 5, 2017, https://www.cnbc.com/2017/05/05/unusual-blank-check-company -began-trading-nyse-for-first-time.html.

4. Phil Mackintosh, "A Record Pace for SPACs in 2021," NASDAQ (website), January 6, 2022, https://www.nasdaq.com/articles/a-record -pace-for-spacs-in-2021.

5. Sujeet Indap and Mark Vandevelde, "Private Equity: Apollo's Lucrative But Controversial Bet on Insurance," *The Financial Times*, October 31, 2018, https://www.ft.com/content/a7cb24ec-cae9-11e8 -9fe5-24ad351828ab.

6. Greg Iacurci, "Annuity Sales Hit Record Last Year, Eclipsing Sales During 2008 Financial Crisis Amid Fear, Higher Rates," CNBC (website), February 2, 2023, https://www.cnbc.com/2023/02/02/annuity-sales-record-2022-higher-interest-rates-stock-market-recession-fear.html.

CONCLUSION: THE PROMISE OF PRIVATE CAPITAL

1. Sam McCartney, "Can Private Equity Outperformance Persist?" Marquette Associates (website), June 24, 2021, https://www.marquetteassociates.com/wp-content/uploads/2021/05/Can-Private-Equity-Outperformance-Persist.pdf.
2. Robert F. Smith, "Why Asset Managers Could Be the Unlikely Heroes Who Drive Social, Cultural, and Economic Impact at Scale," *Fortune*, January 24, 2023, https://fortune.com/2023/01/24/asset-managers-unlikely-heroes-social-cultural-economic-impact-scale-robert-f-smith/.
3. Smith, "Why Asset Managers."
4. Bain & Company, *Global Private Equity Report 2023*, 58, accessed March 3, 2023, https://www.bain.com/globalassets/noindex/2023/bain_report_global-private-equity-report-2023.pdf.
5. Isadore Barmash, "Tiffany's Sale Set to Executives," *New York Times*, August 31, 1984, https://www.nytimes.com/1984/08/31/business/tiffany-s-sale-set-to-executives.html.
6. Alison Leigh Cowan, "Big Investor in Household Names," *New York Times*, April 26, 1990, https://www.nytimes.com/1990/04/26/business/big-investor-in-household-names.html.
7. "Locust, Pocus," *The Economist*, May 5, 2005, https://www.economist.com/special-report/2005/05/05/locust-pocus.

INDEX